SYLVIA PORTER'S PERSONAL FINANCE™ GUIDES

Financial Planning

Grolier Enterprises Corp.

SYLVIA PORTER'S PERSONAL FINANCE GUIDES are prepared by Sylvia Porter's Personal Finance Magazine Co. and published by Grolier Enterprises Corp.

Sylvia Porter's Personal Finance Magazine

Sylvia Porter, Editor-in-Chief
Carole Sinclair, Publisher and Editorial Director
Patricia Schiff Estess, Editor

Editor for these guides:
Arthur H. Rogoff

Principal contributors to this guide:
Arthur H. Rogoff (including worksheets), Nellie Sabin, Pàtricia Schiff Estess, Janis Graham and Ellen Hermanson

Grolier Enterprises Corp.

Robert B. Clarke, Publisher

Staff for these guides:
Kenneth W. Leish, Editor-in-Chief
Bernard M. Garfinkel, Senior Editor
Don Longabucco, Art Director
Susan Stellingwerf, Editorial Assistant
Margaret M. Fina, Production Manager

Photograph on cover and page 5 by Alex Gotfryd

Published by Grolier Enterprises Corp.

ISBN: 0-7172-8175-2

This book is intended to provide general information and background and is distributed on the basis that the publisher and copyright owner are not engaged in rendering legal, accounting, or other professional services. Should legal, accounting, or other professional assistance be required, the services of a competent professional should be sought. The publisher, copyright owner, and authors disclaim any personal liability for advice or information presented herein.

Library of Congress Catalog Card Number: 85-070393

Printed in the United States of America

Contents

Taking control of your finances could be the most important financial decision you make in your life. "Financial planning" may sound intimidating, but you'll discover that it is basically an extension of many things you already do. If you've opened a savings account or an IRA, bought stocks or U.S. savings bonds, or asked for a raise, you've been managing your finances. Personal financial planning is simply a comprehensive, organized approach to this vital activity.

When it comes to financial planning, good intentions are not enough. Everyone needs a financial plan to keep pace with the changes that naturally occur in life. A good financial plan is flexible. It provides you with a way to take care of your financial "present" at the same time that you build the secure financial future that should be your goal.

Sylvia Porter

Introduction: How to Plan Your Financial Future

There is a good reason why this book comes to you as the first volume of Sylvia Porter's Personal Finance Guides. Financial planning is the most sensible way for you to control your financial future, and it should play a major role in all of your financial decisions.

What is financial planning? Think of it as a road map, marked to show you the right routes to follow, the right turns to make as you travel through your financial lifetime. *Financial Planning* tells you, step by step, how to prepare such a map—a comprehensive, lifetime financial planning program based on three essential factors: *where you are, where you want to go, and how you can get there.*

You begin by making a detailed analysis of your present financial situation. *This is where you are.*

You complete the financial planning worksheets that are an integral part of the book. They enable you to identify your most vital financial goals and calculate exactly how much money over how many years you will need to accomplish these goals. *This is where you want to go.* (Most of the worksheets in the book have been filled out as samples for you to follow as you complete the blank forms provided for you in the *Financial Record Book.*)

You combine your individual goals into a unified financial planning program. *That is how you can get there.*

As it guides you through this process, this book describes the nature and basic principles of financial planning. It provides the expert information you need to make wise decisions on the many aspects of personal finance that are involved in financial planning, from personal money management and investment to sheltering income from taxation and planning for a financially secure retirement. And it offers specific advice on handling the major events in your life—from getting married to changing careers—that can affect your financial planning program.

At the same time, *Financial Planning* serves as an introduction to the other books in the Personal Finance series, directing you toward more extensive coverage of subjects that are treated in this volume mainly as they relate to financial planning.

Financial Planning and all of the other volumes in Sylvia Porter's Personal Finance Guides have one purpose: to supply you with the knowledge you need to plan and build a sound financial future. If you think about what that can mean, you'll realize that you are about to begin an exciting—and highly productive—endeavor.

I. Establishing a Financial Planning Program

Some Personal Guidelines

Financial planning requires a commitment in time and energy. Here are some guidelines to keep in mind as you start out:

1) Begin by recognizing that lifetime financial planning is as important to your general well-being as physical fitness.
2) Set aside a period of time for financial planning involving you and your spouse—and, if you like, your older children. These sessions should become a regular part of your schedule.
3) Become more knowledgeable. Follow personal finance coverage through the media and make use of computer software, cassettes, seminars, and educational courses.
4) Consult with qualified financial planners, bankers, stockbrokers, and other advisers as the need arises.
5) Keep your planning relatively simple, even after you become more knowledgeable and consult with professional advisers.

How Financial Planning Works

Preparing your own financial planning program essentially involves collecting information about your present financial situation and your future financial goals. Here is how this process will work as you proceed through this book:

Figuring Out Where You Are. Your entire program of financial planning must be based on a realistic appraisal of your assets and liabilities and your income and expenses. That is the purpose of the first two worksheets, "Current Statement of Income and Expenses" (Worksheet 1) and "Current Financial Statement and Inventory" (Worksheet 2). The time and effort you invest in completing these worksheets (and the others in the book) will be repaid in full as a clear picture of your present and future financial situation emerges.

Figuring Out Where You Want To Go. You'll do this by identifying specific financial goals and using the worksheets to calculate how much money you must save/invest to accomplish them. You will also need to adjust your goals from time to time in response to changes in your life, such as getting a new job (*see page 11*).

Your goals may include financing your children's college education, buying a home, planning your retirement, protecting yourself and your family against catastrophic medical expenses, and providing for your family in case of death.

Certain goals, such as children's college educations, might be long-term ones, to be realized in five or ten or more years. Others, such as owning a home, might be intermediate goals, achieved in one to five years. Still others, like buying a new car, might be short-term, achieved within a year. You'll find that setting and achieving short-term goals will encourage you to propose and work toward achieving intermediate- and long-term ones.

Figuring Out How You Can Get There. When you have completed all the worksheets, you will have identified and put a price tag on your goals. You can then integrate them into a workable, unified plan of financial action—your financial planning program. The final section of the book, "Putting It All Together," shows you how to do this.

Now you are ready to take the first step in preparing your financial planning program. Look at Worksheets 1 and 2. Gather together the data you will need for these worksheets, and complete them on the blank forms provided in the *Financial Record Book*.

FINANCIAL PLANNING WORKSHEETS

The worksheets in this book have been filled out as samples according to the "Smith family" profile described below. The worksheets illustrate how financial planning works for this family. In preparing their own worksheets, readers will obtain results that reflect their own circumstances.

To complete Worksheets 1 and 2, prepare detailed listings of necessary information. Record the totals from these listings on the worksheets, and attach the listings to the worksheets for future reference.

Smith Family Profile

Mr. Smith, age 35, has worked for 18 years for a company that sells and services office machines and equipment, including, as of the past five years, computers and other advanced systems.

Mrs. Smith, age 28, worked as a teacher until four years ago.

Savings/Investment

The Smiths have been married for seven years. Mr. Smith started working for his company when he graduated from high school at a salary of $10,000. He completed two years of college in evenings. His salary is now $30,000. Mrs. Smith's salary increased from $15,000 to $18,000 during her working years. They have saved and invested about 5% of their annual incomes, producing an average annual return after taxes of slightly more than 6%.

Future Plans

1. The Smiths have one child, age four, and plan to have another in two years. They are planning college educations for both children.
2. They plan to buy/build a home when their second child is in first grade, about eight years from now.
3. Mrs. Smith would like to establish her own retail business in five years, when the children are nine and three years old.
4. The Smiths have set aside $39,500, acquired by savings/investment. Of this, $26,000 is slated for short and medium term objectives, excluding retirement. The remaining $13,500 is reserved for a financial emergency and represents five months' total expenses, including taxes.

Worksheet 1

CURRENT STATEMENT OF INCOME AND EXPENSES

	Year:
INCOME	
Total employment income	$30,000
Self-employment income	
Profits from business/partnership	
Interest, dividends, rents, royalties, fees	2,100
Child support and alimony received	
Social Security, pensions, annuities	
Other	
TOTAL INCOME	$32,100
EXPENSES	
Debts	
Principal and interest on:	
Residential mortgages	
Investment mortgages	
Loans, notes, margin accounts	
Balances due on installment payments	$1,000
Payments on borrowings from your employer or benefit plans	
Other	
TOTAL PAYMENTS ON DEBTS	1,000
Taxes	
Federal income taxes	4,140
State and local income taxes	1,500
Social Security contributions	2,010
Residential real estate	
Investment real estate	
Other	
TOTAL TAXES	7,650
Living Expenses	
Food and beverages at home	5,000
Food and beverages away from home	2,000
Household supplies	1,000
Housing, maintenance, utilities	5,100
Clothing (purchases and care)	1,500
Transportation (including autos, gas)	1,800
Insurance premiums	1,500
Entertainment, recreation, vacations	1,000
Medical and other health expenses (unreimbursed)	1,100
Contributions, donations, gifts	500
Education and day care	
Child support and alimony paid	
Grooming and other personal care	1,300
Other (pets, legal, accounting, etc.)	
TOTAL LIVING EXPENSES	21,800
TOTAL EXPENSES	$30,450
POSITIVE (NET) CASH FLOW	
TOTAL INCOME LESS TOTAL EXPENSES	$1,650
INTO SAVINGS	
INTO INVESTMENTS	$1,650

Worksheet 2

CURRENT FINANCIAL STATEMENT AND INVENTORY

	Date:
ASSETS	
Liquid Assets (Readily Convertible to Cash)	
Cash and checking; savings; money market accounts; CDs	$5,200
Money market mutual funds	5,600
Cash in stockbrokerage accounts	
U.S. savings bonds	2,200
Cash value of life insurance, annuities, employee benefit plans	2,100
Other	
TOTAL LIQUID ASSETS	15,100
Marketable Investments	
Stocks	9,300
Corporate bonds, government securities	2,000
Stock/bond mutual funds	15,200
Options, futures, commodities, precious metals	
Other	
TOTAL MARKETABLE INVESTMENTS	26,500
"Nonmarketable" Investments	
IRAs, Keoghs	10,500
Real estate	
Tax shelters	
Deferred employment income	
Vested interests in employee benefits	2,200
Business interests/partnerships	
Loans to others	
Collectibles for investment	
Trust funds	
Other	
TOTAL "NONMARKETABLE" INVESTMENTS	12,700
Personal Assets	
Residential real estate	
Autos, other vehicles	2,700
Jewelry, furs, furnishings, personal collectibles	3,500
Other	
TOTAL PERSONAL ASSETS	6,200
TOTAL ASSETS	$60,500
LIABILITIES	
Charge account, credit card balances	250
Other bills to be paid	140
Mortgages on residential and investment real estate	
Loans, notes, margin accounts	
Balance due on installment payments	1,650
Borrowed from your employer or against employee benefit plans	
Estimated liability for income taxes	
Other	
TOTAL LIABILITIES	$2,040
NET WORTH TOTAL ASSETS LESS TOTAL LIABILITIES	$58,460

II. *Financial Factors Triggered by Life Experiences*

Adjusting Financial Factors

When you have completed Worksheets 1 and 2, you'll see that they represent in graphic form "where you are." But you must be aware that your circumstances will change from time to time. Sometimes these changes will require relatively simple financial adjustments, such as when two working people marry or live together and both continue working. At other times, more elaborate financial planning will be necessary.

Refer to the chart, "Financial Planning for Life Experiences" on page 12. You can use this chart to keep track of your changing life experiences and check off the financial factors you have to adjust as each change occurs.

First, look at the column "Life Experiences." You may not experience all of these eventualities in your life. You might, for instance, be single "On Your Own," not "Living Together." But the ones you do experience will surely be major turning points for you.

Next, look across the top of the checklist at the heading "Financial Factors." As you will note, these factors are grouped into five areas—Planning, Employment, Money Management, Insurance, and Investment by Objectives. Together, they represent the major financial elements every person must control. If you change one, it usually will have an effect on one or more of the others.

For example, if your career advances, your income will increase and you will want to protect some of your newfound dollars from higher taxes. You might begin investing in tax-advantaged securities, such as municipal bonds or tax-shelter limited partnerships instead of putting some of your additional earnings into savings and some into taxable securities such as corporate bonds. If you did, this move would affect various financial factors, including "Budgeting" (more after-tax dollars available), "Taxes," "Savings," "Earnings," "Investments," and "Tax Benefits."

The point is, you'll need to reshape your financial situation as you undergo new life experiences. Basically, this involves adjusting the five major financial areas. The essence of financial planning is to anticipate, not simply react to, your changing circumstances. If you have prepared in advance for change, it will be far easier for you to make the necessary financial adjustments.

FINANCIAL PLANNING FOR LIFE EXPERIENCES

		Financial Factors															
		1. Planning			2. Employment		3. Money Management			4. Insurance				5. Investment by Objective			
	LIFE EXPERIENCES	Budgeting	Taxes	Inflation	Earnings	Employment Benefits	Checking and Savings	Credit and Borrowing	Government Programs	Health	Disability	Life	Property and Liability	Income	Growth	Appreciation	Tax Benefits
1	ON YOUR OWN																
2	LIVING TOGETHER																
3	YOU GET MARRIED																
4	YOU HAVE CHILDREN																
5	YOU BUY YOUR FIRST HOME																
6	YOUR CAREER ADVANCES																
7	YOUR CHILDREN GO TO COLLEGE																
8	YOUR CHILDREN LEAVE HOME																
9	SPOUSE RETURNS TO WORK																
10	ADVERSITIES																
11	DIVORCE																
12	REMARRIAGE																
13	UPGRADING YOUR LIFESTYLE																
14	CARING FOR AN AGING PARENT																
15	A NEW CAREER IN MIDLIFE																
16	RETIREMENT																
17	DEATH IN THE FAMILY																

Use a chart like this as a checklist to keep track of financial factors that need adjustment because of changing life experiences. In response to a changed life experience, check relevant boxes, then adjust relevant worksheet(s).

In this section, you'll see how you can use these financial factors as tools in adjusting your financial planning. In every case, as you undergo a new life experience, your aim is to make sure that your financial plan reflects your changed circumstances. To do so, you need continuously to revise and update your financial planning so that it takes into account the new experience. Section III will cover various life experiences and show how to apply these financial factors to them.

Financial Factor #1: Planning

Budgeting. You can't plan your financial present and future effectively without creating a budget and sticking to it.

Creating a Budget. Look at Worksheet 1, "Current Statement of Income and Expenses," which you've already prepared. This is the basis for your present annual budget. Does it show a positive cash flow of total income that is larger than total expenses? If it doesn't, you are in financial trouble.

There is only one solution to this problem: You must work out a stringent budget, either by yourself or with professional counseling help. You should consider consolidating your debts to facilitate monthly repayment. And above all, you must commit yourself to following the budget you've devised.

If you're in the happier situation of showing a positive or net cash flow in Worksheet 1, you can begin to create your budget, using Worksheet 3, "Your Budget," as your guide.

- First, break down the annual figures for each line item in Worksheet 1 into the period you prefer—weekly (divide by 52), monthly (divide by 12), or quarterly (divide by 4). Monthly works best for most people because that's when they pay their bills.

  Your income and expenses will fluctuate, of course. An annual bonus and quarterly dividends, for example, would increase some months' income over others. The solution is to calculate your yearly totals and put monthly installments for extra costs into savings until these expenses are due. This breakdown should be entered in the column "Expected This Month" in Worksheet 3.
- Second, classify the expenses in Worksheet 1 into two categories, fixed and variable. Fixed expenses include payments on debts, insurance premiums, rent or mortgage payments. You probably can't do much to reduce them. Variable expenses include food, clothing, entertainment, and recreation. You may be able to reduce your variable expenses, thus increasing your net cash flow. (See chart, page 15, which shows recommended percentages for various incomes and budget categories.)

It is vitally important to define clearly and budget your net cash flow, since it is the basis for the funds you want to accumulate to accomplish your goals. Any reductions in expenses and increases in income that you are able to effect will be reflected in the "Budgeted Revision" column in Worksheet 3. Use the "Actual" column to record your actual expenses, then compare these to the "Budgeted Revision" to check on how well you are adhering to your budget.

Sticking to Your Budget. *The key to making your budget work is devising one to fit your income and lifestyle.* Everyone goes off a budget once in a while; don't feel guilty if you do. Get right back on it.

Taxes. No one needs to be reminded that taxes have an important effect on income and expenses and, thus, on budget and financial planning. Income taxes comprise by far the largest portion of taxes you pay. Here's how to handle them for budgeting purposes:

1) Whether or not you are required to pay quarterly estimated taxes, estimate the coming year's income, deductions, credits, and exemptions for your budget and financial planning. (Follow Worksheet 4. "Estimating Your Federal Income Taxes.")
2) Revise your estimated taxes—and, therefore, your budget and planning—for any significant changes that take place.
3) Keep proper records throughout the year. Having full details readily available makes it easier for you to prepare returns.

Worksheet 3

YOUR BUDGET (January)						
	EXPECTED THIS MONTH	BUDGETED REVISION	ACTUAL	ACTUAL VS. BUDGETED		
				+	−	
INCOME						
(itemized and total)	______	______	______			______
FIXED EXPENSES						
(itemized and total)	______	______	______			______
VARIABLE EXPENSES						
(itemized and total)	______	______	______			______
TOTAL EXPENSES	______	______	______			______
NET CASH FLOW						
(total income less						
total expenses)	______	______	______			______
—INTO SAVINGS	______	______	______			______
—INTO INVESTMENTS	______	______	______			______
NET CASH FLOW APPORTIONED TO SPECIFIC GOALS						
1. College education	______					
2. Vacation trip	______					
3. ______________	______					

FOUR REPRESENTATIVE BUDGETS
(Figures represent % of income)

BUDGET ITEMS	1	2	3	4
Housing and ultilities	24	25	23	15
Food	11	10	15	15
Laundry and clothing	4	4	5	3
Personal care	2	2	2	2
Medical	1	2	4	5
Transportation	14	7	8	17
Leisure	10	5	5	4
Insurance	2	3	2	3
Savings and investment	3	5	3	1
Miscellaneous	7	5	3	14
Income taxes and pay deductions	22	32	30	21

1—Single, early 20s, income $20,000 a year.
2—Couple, late 30s, one works, income $40,000 a year.
3—Family, middle 40s, 1 child, both work, income $50,000 a year.
4—Couple, late 60s, both retired, income $30,000 a year.

Inflation. Your financial planning should take into account the possible effects of inflation. Note Table A, page 26, "Calculating Annual Rates of Inflation and of Return," which is to be used in preparing Worksheets 5, 6, 7, 8, and 11.

Financial Factor #2: Employment

The work you do is, of course, the backbone of your financial life, since it usually produces the major portion of your income. The two aspects of this financial factor, earnings and employment benefits, are discussed fully in Section III in relation to the relevant life experience, Employment, beginning on page 23.

Financial Factor #3: Money Management

Checking and Savings. Since your budgeting makes provision for diverting part of your net cash flow—income less expenses—into savings and part into investments, you should pay careful attention to your checking and savings accounts. Your objectives are to obtain maximum interest and pay minimum fees.

A wide variety of accounts are available. These include NOW (negotiable order of withdrawal) and Super NOW accounts, which are interest-bearing checking accounts; passbook savings accounts; money market deposit accounts, which also afford limited checking privileges; certificates of deposit (CDs), which are interest-bearing deposits that mature at a specific time; and sweep accounts, which are

Worksheet 4

ESTIMATING YOUR FEDERAL INCOME TAXES	LAST YEAR	THIS YEAR
INCOME		
Salaries and wages	$29,000	$30,000
Interest and dividends less exclusion	1,950	2,100
Net business/partnership income (loss)		
Net long-term capital gains (losses)	350	450
Other net gains (losses)		
Other income (loss)		
TOTAL GROSS INCOME	$31,300	$32,550
ADJUSTMENTS		
Less:		
IRA contributions	$ 2,250	$ 2,250
Keogh contributions		
Unreimbursed business expenses		
Alimony paid		
Other adjustments		
ADJUSTED GROSS INCOME	$29,050	$30,300
DEDUCTIONS AND EXEMPTIONS:		
Deductions if you itemize (above zero bracket amount already deducted in tax tables)		
Exemptions	$ 3,000	$ 3,000
TAXABLE INCOME	$26,060	$27,300
ESTIMATED TAX PAYABLE	$ 4,030	$ 4,140
Less tax credits		
Add other taxes		
ESTIMATED NET TAXES	4,030	4,140
WITHHELD	$ 4,000	$ 4,100
ESTIMATED QUARTERLY TAX PAYMENTS		

Note: Revisions in the federal tax laws, if adopted, might change the way in which you estimate your taxes.

interest-bearing checking accounts that "sweep" amounts over a specified level into higher-interest accounts. When the sweep account balance drops below a minimum requirement, money from another account is swept into the checking account. (Credit unions offer similar accounts under other names.)

In addition, stock brokerage firms offer multiple asset management accounts under various proprietary names, and these provide many of the services mentioned above. Some mutual fund management companies also provide the equivalent of multiple asset management accounts. And most of these companies offer money market, bond, tax-exempt, and other types of mutual funds that include check-writing privileges.

All the accounts mentioned have varying requirements for minimum deposits and balances. Which one(s) you choose to open will depend on your particular financial situation.

Savings are a vital part of your financial planning program. Your budgeting should provide ways for you to save some of your income, as a reserve for emergencies and to fuel the money growth that will fund your goals. An essential point to keep in mind is that steady savings and compound interest produce extraordinary growth.

For further information on banks and bank accounts, see Sylvia Porter's Personal Finance Guide, *Personal Banking*.

Credit and Loans. Over the years, you will borrow money for many reasons and in varying ways. The key to managing credit is simple: Don't overextend yourself. Follow these credit rules:

1. Never borrow unless you have a good prospect for repayment.
2. Never borrow to buy impulsively or to boost your morale.
3. Never use credit to increase your daily standard of living without having the financial resources to sustain such an increase. Ultimately your bills will come due.
4. Never borrow to speculate on risky ventures.

WHERE TO BORROW

Loans and credit can be obtained from commercial banks, S&Ls, savings banks, credit unions, small loan companies, insurance companies, stock brokerage firms, employers, executive loan services, and pawn shops. Credit is extended by merchants and credit card systems. If you borrow from relatives or friends, it's important to both parties that the loan be arranged as a business transaction. The worst way to borrow is from loan sharks.

TYPES OF CREDIT AND LOANS

These are some of the kinds of credit and loans available:

Unsecured (no collateral) cash loans; secured loans (you put up collateral such as a savings account); overdraft loans (you can write checks for more than the amount you have on deposit); ready credit bank lines approved in advance of your needs; passbook and money market accounts and CD loans; home mortgage, second mortgage, and mortgage refinancing loans; billed-payment and revolving credit charge accounts; credit card loans; life insurance policy loans; auto loans; stock brokerage margin accounts (the broker loans you money to buy securities); loans from employers; and loans taken against funds accumulated in retirement and other benefits accounts.

EVALUATING LENDERS

To evaluate money-lending sources, shop around and compare interest rates, total financing charges, length of loans, repayment periods, number of payments, penalties, and other factors. Lenders quote interest rates in different ways, which can make comparison difficult. Don't let them confuse you. The Truth in Lending Act requires the disclosure of true interest—the annual percentage rate (APR).

ESTABLISHING A GOOD CREDIT RATING

To establish a good credit rating, you must pass the "Three Cs" of the credit test that lenders use to determine who is a good credit risk and who isn't.

1. **Character:** How honest and trustworthy are you? Do you have a record of paying your bills on time?
2. **Capacity:** What is your financial ability to repay the loan?
3. **Capital:** Do you have any assets such as bank accounts or a home, that can be used as backing in case you default?

It's useful to establish a good credit record even if you don't have a current need to borrow money. Lenders usually refer your application to credit reporting bureaus for credit information on you. Under the Fair Credit Reporting Act, you have the right to review your file at a credit bureau. It is wise to review such files periodically since they may contain unjustified adverse information that could be used to turn down your application for credit.

Here's how to establish a good credit rating:

- Don't let your checking accounts become overdrawn. Make deposits regularly into savings accounts even if each deposit is a small amount. Build up other assets, and pay your bills on time.
- Start borrowing, even if you don't have to. Begin by using store charge accounts, then add credit cards, then borrow a nominal sum from a bank. These moves may cost you interest, but if they do, it will be money well spent in establishing a good credit rating. To solidify your rating, step up the amounts of money involved.

Note: Credit ratings and credit reports are vital elements of money management. These subjects and other aspects of credit are discussed extensively in Sylvia Porter's Personal Finance Guides, *Personal Banking* and *Borrowing Money*.

TIPS ON REDUCING YOUR COSTS WHEN BORROWING

- Where applicable, make as large a down payment as possible to reduce the amount you need to borrow.
- Schedule repayments over the shortest period possible.

- Secure loans that permit accelerated payments with no penalty or a minimum penalty. But don't accelerate payments if you have loans at low interest rates. Better to invest your extra cash and earn higher interest.
- Generally, it's better not to take out credit life and credit accident insurance tied in with a loan because these kinds of insurance typically cost more than separate policies.
- Keep in mind that interest payments are usually tax deductible.

GOVERNMENT PROGRAMS

Among the wide range of federal, state, and local government programs that may affect your personal financial planning are:

- **Social Security.** Keep in mind that Social Security is not just a retirement income. It's life insurance protection that can be worth thousands of dollars to young families. It is also disability protection, since it pays benefits to a worker who has permanently or indefinitely prolonged disabilities.

  The Social Security record-keeping system is not infallible. Your earnings could end up in someone else's account or fail to be recorded at all. To check, mail in the form, "Request for Social Security Statement of Earnings," available at your local Social Security office.
- **Commercial.** If you're interested in starting or expanding a business, there are various government agencies that can be helpful, including the U.S. Department of Commerce and the Small Business Administration.
- **Others.** These include Medicare, Medicaid, worker's compensation, educational funding, and unemployment compensation.

For further discussion of money management, consult Sylvia Porter's Personal Finance Guide, *Personal Banking*.

Financial Factor #4: Insurance

Various kinds of insurance are discussed in Section III in conjunction with relevant life experiences. For "Health," see page 48, for "Disability," see page 43, for "Life Insurance," see page 50.

Financial Factor #5: Investment by Objective

Objectives. The four primary objectives in an investment program are income, growth, appreciation (distinguished from growth because it is shorter-term with rapid growth), and tax benefits. Any investments you make for one of these primary objectives may also accomplish one or more of the other objectives. For example, you may invest in a mutual fund whose primary objective is income but which also affords some growth. Or you may invest in a growth stock that also provides some income. Generally, investments that are made primarily for income are relatively conservative. Those made for growth are somewhat riskier, and those made for appreciation are still more speculative.

You will increase your potential risk and reward by leveraging your investments, that is, buying in part with your own money and in part with funds borrowed from your broker. With securities, this is known as buying "on margin." The degree of potential risk and reward will increase in proportion to the amount of borrowed funds. The leveraged portion increases your gain over your cash investment if the return exceeds the interest you pay on the borrowed funds. But it substantially increases your loss if the decline in value plus the interest you pay are more than any income you receive.

Your personal circumstances at the time—plus your risk tolerance—will dictate your objectives. Your primary objective may be income if you've had a baby, bought a home, a child starts college, you have to help ailing parents, or you're retiring. If your working income has increased sharply, if you've received a bonus, an inheritance or other windfall, or if all your children are now on their own, your principal objective might be growth or appreciation or tax liability reduction.

Risk Tolerance. You can get some idea of your risk tolerance by responding to the following statements. Make your selection on the basis of which statement you would generally be most comfortable with.

A. I want maximum safety—I don't want to risk any loss.

B. I'll take a small amount of risk for a higher potential return.

C. I'll take medium risk for potentially greater reward.

D. I'm willing to speculate and take substantial risk of losses for possible maximum gains.

Once you have some idea of your general risk temperament, you may want to apply this knowledge to your investment program by assigning percentage values to different objectives. For example, if your risk tolerance and your income are relatively high, you might want to adopt the following investment program:

(A) Income: 20%; (B) Growth: 30%; (C) Appreciation: 30%; (D) Tax Benefits: 20%.

In evaluating your risk tolerance, you should consider how liquid your prospective investments are, that is, how readily you can obtain the funds you put into them.

Money market funds, for example, provide great liquidity, while tax-shelter limited partnerships, for example, are long-term commitments that lack liquidity. You also have to consider an investment in terms of its ease of management. Do you want to pursue do-it-yourself investing by buying individual securities? Would you rather invest within a group framework by buying mutual funds? Or do you want a combination of these approaches?

DOING IT YOURSELF

Here are some useful guidelines if you want to buy individual stocks, bonds, and other securities:

- Become knowledgeable about the market and the securities you want to buy. Invest your time before you invest your money.
- Seek the advice of experts, to get more specifics and a broader overview. But remember that experts can be fallible, too.
- Be leery of rumors and tips.
- Be aware of the risks you're getting into. Don't invest in situations not compatible with your risk tolerance.
- Don't expect too much too soon. On the other hand, don't become overly attached to an investment—constantly reappraise it.
- Fit each investment into an overall plan. Otherwise you'll wind up with an investment mix that doesn't meet your particular needs.
- Diversify. Don't put all your eggs in one basket.
- Don't expect every investment to work out exactly as you expected. Learn from your mistakes, and try not to repeat them.

INVESTING WITHIN A GROUP FRAMEWORK

Here are some opportunities for investment in a group framework:

Mutual Funds. These are investment companies with diversified investment portfolios. Among the advantages they provide are: professional management, the ability to invest small amounts, diversification, convenience, and liquidity (you can convert your shares quickly into cash).

Closed-End Funds. Unlike mutual funds, closed-end funds have a fixed number of shares which are bought and sold through stockbrokers on stock exchanges or the over-the-counter market.

Unit Trusts. When you buy a share in a unit trust, you own a piece of a diversified portfolio, as is the case with mutual funds and closed-end funds. But unlike the funds, whose investments change, unit trusts are formed with unchanging portfolio holdings.

Investment Limited Partnerships. These are commonly known as tax shelters. Some seek maximum tax write-offs (in early years or long term). Others stress income, capital gains, or combinations of tax advantages, income, and capital gains.

Investment Clubs. Most investment clubs have 10 to 20 members who agree to invest a set amount—often as little as $25—each month. Members then meet regularly to plan their investments.

Other Factors. Keep in mind these factors as you plan your investment program:

Before you start investing, protect yourself in two ways:

1) Keep enough money in savings accounts to cover your living expenses for from three to six months in case of emergencies.
2) Make sure that you have an adequate amount of insurance.

You should be aware also that owning your own home represents a large and important investment (*see page 33*).

And you should consider, on a priority basis, investing in an Individual Retirement Account (IRA), which defers income taxes on up to $2,000 per year from employment income. A working spouse may also contribute $2,000 a year in a separate account. A working and non-working spouse can contribute up to $2,250 a year in separate accounts, provided that not more than $2,000 is put into any one account.

Similarly, if you and your spouse have income from self-employment, you should invest through a Keogh plan, which is similar to an IRA but defers a portion of *self-employment* income from taxation. Other tax-benefit plans are available, often through your employer, including pension, profit-sharing, savings, thrift, employee stock ownership plans (ESOPs), and tax-deferred compensation plans. You should take advantage of them to the greatest extent possible.

Keep in mind that each year's contributions do not have to go into the IRA or Keogh you set up in prior years. You should consider starting new plans each year—plans that represent different types of investments that may be more appropriate for your changed circumstances. Consider also switching funds accumulated in prior years to different types of Keoghs and IRAs. You want to get the best return possible while safely preserving your money for retirement.

For further information on investment, consult Sylvia Porter's Personal Finance Guide, *An Introduction to Investing in Stocks and Bonds*.

III. Life Experiences

In this section, you'll learn how to use the financial factors to shape your financial planning in response to specific life experiences. These life experiences are grouped into the major areas of Employment, Changing Relationships, Children, Home, Lifestyle, Adversities, Retirement, and Estate Planning. Use the accompanying worksheets to guide you through the process of allocating and re-allocating your financial resources to accomplish your financial goals.

Life Experience: Employment

Most people receive substantially greater funds from their work than from all other sources. Income from work can easily exceed a million dollars during a person's career. Work also usually provides insurance protection, retirement income, and other benefits greater than the total from any other sources.

Advancing Your Career. Your career will probably involve a substantial number of these eight situations: getting an education, advancing within a single company, changing employers, changing careers, starting a sideline business, starting a full-time business, changing careers in mid-life, working after retirement.

Employers. There are advantages to staying with the same employer for many years or even throughout your work life. It may be easier to advance within the company and to amass generous fringe benefits, particularly through retirement programs. On the other hand, if your old employer tends to take your good work for granted, you may sharply increase your compensation by moving to a new job.

Income should not be your only consideration when changing jobs. Consider also such factors as the success and prospects for growth of the respective companies, the type of work you are doing, the location, and the opportunity for future advancement.

Starting Your Own Business. You have to weigh carefully many factors before you risk your life's savings, commit yourself to repaying borrowed funds, or give up your present job's income and fringe benefits to go into your own business. This is true whether you're thinking of a full-time business or moonlighting in a sideline business, whether you'll need a business location or will be operating from your home. Here are the kinds of questions you'll need to answer:

- Are you the entrepreneurial type? Do you have the right background and temperament to run your own business?
- Do you have or can you acquire the management ability to operate a business successfully?

- How feasible is the business? Have you, or an expert you've retained, gathered, sorted, analyzed, and evaluated all the information you need to answer that question?
- Are you prepared for the long hours, hard work, responsibilities, stress, and loneliness that are usually required?
- Do you and your family understand what will be involved? In particular, are you and they prepared to lower your standard of living for several months or even years? Or to fail?

There are three basic ways you might be going into business. One, you might acquire a going business or an interest in it. Two, you might set up a business that is part of a network, linked to many related businesses offering the same products or services, such as a franchise or cooperative. Three, the most difficult approach, you might start a new business from scratch. (See Sylvia Porter's Personal Finance Guide, *Starting Your Own Business*.)

DRAWING UP A BUSINESS PLAN

In any case, you'll need a business plan to pinpoint where you are going and how you are going to get there. To begin with, the business plan will indicate how much money you'll need to get started, including money you have obtained from lenders, creditors, or investors. (Complete Worksheet 5, "Funding Your Own Business," using Tables A and B on pages 26 and 27.)

The business plan will also indicate how much money you'll need to operate, and how it should be allocated. It will include provisions for management, personnel, marketing, record-keeping, equipment, purchasing and inventory management, and production/service operations. And it should present financial information such as budget forecasts, statements of objectives, and steps to reach those goals; credit and collection policies and procedures; and insurance requirements.

In addition to any money you put into the business, you might want to raise additional funds by selling equity—that is, shares of ownership—or by borrowing through loans or credit, or by using a combination of equity and debt. You probably will have to secure borrowed funds with some of your personal assets. This could substantially affect your assets and net worth (Worksheet 2). Alternatively, capital may be furnished to your business in the form of extended credit. In this case, you might buy a business, franchise, or equipment and merchandise and pay the seller in installments.

Your Career Advances. You've been promoted, you've started a higher-paying job, your business is finally in the black. Your increased income calls for three financial moves:

Worksheet 5

FUNDING YOUR OWN BUSINESS

1. AMOUNT NEEDED IN TODAY'S DOLLARS:	
a. To acquire a going business, a franchise or other network business, or a business started from scratch. . .	$30,000
b. Add required working capital and reserves.	10,000
c. Subtract funds supplied from other sources as equity investment, loan, or combination of equity and loan. . . .	30,000
d. Amount of your own contribution in today's dollars.	10,000
2. ADJUSTMENT FOR INFLATION:	
a. How many years from now will you need this amount? .	5
b. Estimate average annual rate of inflation between now and then.	6%
c. Refer to Table A. Enter factor obtained by intersecting years and inflation %.	1.34
d. Multiply amount of your own funds 1.d. by factor 2.c. This gives you amount needed *adjusted for inflation*. . .	($10,000 x 1.34) $13,400
3. ESTIMATED RETURN ON INVESTMENT:	
a. Amount you currently have available in today's dollars. .	$5,000
b. Estimate average annual rate of return on investment. .	8%
c. Refer to Table A. Enter factor obtained by intersecting years 2.a. and % return on investment.	1.47
d. To calculate what your present funds will be worth through investment when you need them, multiply amount available 3.a. by factor 3.c.	($5,000 x 1.47) $7,350
4. SHORTAGE OR OVERAGE IN FUNDS YOU WILL NEED: Subtract 3.d. from 2.d.	($13,400 – 7,350) $6,050
5. IF OVERAGE: Calculate lesser amount you must save/invest to accumulate inflation-adjusted amount 2.d.	
6. IF SHORTAGE, ADDITIONAL INVESTMENT REQUIRED:	
a. Refer to Table B. Enter factor obtained by intersecting years and estimated % return on investment 3.b.	5.9
b. Divide shortage in 4. by factor 6.a.	($6,050 ÷ 5.9) $1,025

This is the additional amount (above funds currently available) that you must save/invest each year to accomplish your goal.

1) **Increasing Your Life Insurance.** This will protect your family's resulting improved lifestyle (see Worksheet 12, ''How Much Life Insurance Do You Need?'').
2) **Investing More Aggressively.** Your career success provides you with more disposable income. You could invest some of this money aggressively with the goal of achieving maximum appre-

Table A

CALCULATING ANNUAL RATES OF INFLATION AND OF RETURN					
END OF YEAR	4%	6%	8%	10%	12%
1	1.04	1.06	1.08	1.10	1.12
2	1.08	1.12	1.17	1.21	1.25
3	1.12	1.19	1.26	1.33	1.40
4	1.17	1.26	1.36	1.46	1.57
5	1.22	1.34	1.47	1.61	1.76
6	1.26	1.42	1.59	1.77	1.97
7	1.32	1.50	1.71	1.95	2.21
8	1.37	1.59	1.85	2.14	2.48
9	1.42	1.69	2.00	2.36	2.77
10	1.48	1.79	2.16	2.59	3.10
11	1.54	1.90	2.33	2.85	3.48
12	1.60	2.01	2.52	3.14	3.90
13	1.66	2.13	2.72	3.45	4.36
14	1.73	2.26	2.94	3.80	4.89
15	1.80	2.40	3.17	4.18	5.47
16	1.87	2.54	3.43	4.60	6.13
17	1.95	2.69	3.70	5.05	6.87
18	2.02	2.85	4.00	5.56	7.69
19	2.11	3.03	4.32	6.12	8.61
20	2.19	3.21	4.67	6.73	9.65
25	2.66	4.29	6.86	10.83	17.00
30	3.24	5.74	10.06	17.45	30.00

WHAT TABLE A IS USED FOR:
This table provides a factor number to be used when you complete Worksheets 5, 6, 7, 8, and 11. The factor number applies to two calculations:
1) To find the dollar amount—adjusted for inflation—that you will need to accomplish a specific financial goal.
2) To find the dollar amount you will have available at a future time from the investment of presently available funds.
Note: As used in Worksheets 5, 6, 7, 8, and 11, rate of return reflects interest, dividends, and other income from savings/investments, plus growth in those savings/investments.

HOW TO USE TABLE A IN FILLING OUT WORKSHEETS 5, 6, 7, 8, AND 11:
a. Select the future year in which you need the funds.
b. Select % column. Percentages apply either to rate of inflation or to rate of return, as indicated on worksheets.
c. Find intersection of year and % column on table. Enter factor number on worksheet.
d. For years and percentages not shown on table, extrapolate factor number. For example, the factor number for *20 years* at *7%* is halfway between 3.21 and 4.67, or 3.94.

ciation. (But don't do this if your risk tolerance is low.)

You might begin by considering opening new IRAs and Keoghs with your additional income. You could also switch any or all of your IRA and Keogh funds of prior years into more aggressive accounts, *but not at the expense of jeopardizing funds you're accumulating for retirement.*

Table B

CALCULATING NEEDED FUTURE SAVINGS/INVESTMENTS						
END OF YEAR	6%	8%	10%	12%	14%	16%
1	1.0	1.0	1.0	1.0	1.0	1.0
2	2.1	2.1	2.1	2.1	2.1	2.2
3	3.2	3.3	3.3	3.4	3.4	3.5
4	4.4	4.5	4.6	4.8	4.9	5.1
5	5.6	5.9	6.1	6.4	6.6	6.9
6	7.0	7.3	7.7	8.1	8.5	9.0
7	8.4	8.9	9.5	10.1	10.7	11.4
8	9.9	10.6	11.4	12.3	13.2	14.2
9	11.5	12.5	13.6	14.8	16.1	17.5
10	13.2	14.5	16.0	17.6	19.3	21.3
11	15.0	16.7	18.5	20.7	23.1	26.0
12	17.0	19.0	21.4	24.1	27.3	31.0
13	19.0	21.5	25.0	28.0	32.1	36.9
14	21.0	24.2	28.0	32.4	37.6	43.7
15	23.3	27.2	31.8	37.3	43.9	51.6
16	24.0	30.3	36.0	42.8	51.0	60.9
17	28.2	33.7	40.6	49.0	59.1	71.6
18	31.0	37.5	45.6	55.8	68.4	84.0
19	33.7	41.5	51.2	63.4	79.0	98.5
20	36.8	45.8	57.3	72.1	91.0	115.2
25	55.0	73.1	98.4	133.3	183.3	255.5
30	79.1	113.1	164.5	241.3	357.4	416.4

WHAT TABLE B IS USED FOR:
This table provides a factor number to be used when you complete Worksheets 5, 6, 7, 8, and 11. The factor number applies to the calculation of the amount you will need to save/invest on an annual basis and at a specified rate of return in order to accomplish a specific financial goal.

HOW TO USE TABLE B FOR WORKSHEETS 5, 6, 7, 8, AND 11:

a. Select the future year in which you will need the funds.
b. Select % column based on your estimate of average annual rate of return you will achieve on your savings/investments.
c. Find intersection of year and % column on table. Enter factor number on worksheet.
d. For years and percentages that do not appear on table, extrapolate factor number. For example, 20 years at 7% equals a factor number halfway between 36.8 and 45.8, or 41.3.

Note: This table does not take into consideration income tax payments on interest, dividends, rents, or other funds received, including those qualifying as capital gains. These tax payments are covered as expenses on Worksheet 2.

The easiest way for you to become more aggressive in your investing is to buy mutual funds or shares of other investment companies managed with the objective of maximum appreciation. You could also switch some of your present investment holdings into these aggressive mutual funds. But keep in mind that when you switch out of one fund into another, you are actually selling the first fund. If you've realized a profit, you have to pay capital gains tax. (However, in tax-qualified retirement plans, such as an IRA or Keogh, taxes on gains realized on mutual funds or any investment are deferred.)

3) **Sheltering Income from Taxes.** If you haven't already done so, you can begin to invest in tax-benefitted investments. There are three principal kinds:

- Tax-deferred investments, such as U.S. Savings Bonds, annuities, universal life insurance, and the exchange of real estate (swapping instead of selling).
- Tax-advantaged securities, such as municipal bonds, dividend tax-free utility stocks, and tax-exempt money market and bond mutual funds.
- Tax shelters, such as real estate in which you invest directly. Consider also tax-shelter limited partnerships, but investigate them carefully before you proceed.

When sheltering income from taxes, keep in mind that the most important aspect of your decision is the inherent value of the investment, not its tax-beneficial features.

If you invest more actively and aggressively, you must work harder at it. Study *The Wall Street Journal,* the business and financial sections of your daily newspapers, business and financial magazines, trade publications, market letters and research reports of stockbrokers, investment advisory publications and services, and other business and financial material. Consider consulting with professional advisers. You might join the American Association of Individual Investors, 612 North Michigan Avenue, Chicago, IL, 60611, a not-for-profit corporation whose offerings and those of local chapters include publications and seminars to help members become more knowledgable investors.

A New Career in Mid-Life. Most Americans who work will change careers at least once, and frequently two or three times in a lifetime. A decision to change careers (not just jobs) may occur at any time. It may be prompted by a sudden event or a long-simmering idea. Disillusionment with your current line of work, a layoff or firing, dissatisfaction with your earnings and future prospects, or a spouse's transfer to another part of the country, can prompt a person into making a long-dreamed-of change. There's really no best time of life to try for a new career. When you're ready is the best time for you.

In an ideal case, you'll take time to decide what would satisfy you financially, intellectually, and perhaps, physically. A new career might include or depend on a new lifestyle. Instead of the nine-to-five routine of working for an employer, you might find yourself working longer hours launching and running your own business. Or you may have had enough of urban life and decide to manage a small business in a quiet country town—or vice versa.

A key step is to examine your goals thoroughly and assess your strengths and weaknesses, enthusiasms and dislikes, skills and interests.

Those hours of reflection will help you determine what strategies will enable you to achieve your goal. You may have to get additional training.

Be aware, too, of long-term planning as you undertake your new direction. You may have only another year or two to be vested in your present employer company's pension plan, for example. Hold on if you can. Years from now, you may be glad you waited.

Concentrate, too, on practical steps to protect you and your family. Don't leave yourself without adequate insurance protection. During a period of transition, you may be able to convert your employer-sponsored group insurance to individual policies or join a combination group plan through an organization.

You'll certainly have to devise a financial strategy to complement your new career plans. Discuss with your family what changing your career will mean to them, both during the transition and through the launching period. (See Sylvia Porter's Personal Finance Guide, *Managing Your Career.)*

Life Experience: Changing Relationships

Living Together. Millions of men and women have chosen to live together rather than marry. Most such couples consist of two wage-earners, so provisions should be made for sharing living expenses. This may include maintaining a joint checking account. Typically, however, each also keeps a separate checking account, charge accounts, and credit cards for personal expenses, medical bills, and the like. (Such couples can't share health insurance policies or file joint tax returns.)

Protecting what belongs to you is just good sense. If you move in together and combine your household property, itemize who brought which household item. If you make new purchases, decide who owns what and keep a list to avoid arguments later.

Marriage. Here are the financial moves you should make if you are going to be married.

1) Refigure your budget to include your joint financial situation. (You will need to redo Worksheets 1 and 2.)
2) Notify all those involved in your finances that your status will be changing.
3) Inform the Social Security Administration of your marriage in order to become eligible for your spouse's benefits.
4) Write—or rewrite—your wills to include the new spouse.
5) If desired, change the woman's name on driver's license, credit cards, charge accounts, and all other identification.
6) Include your spouse as beneficiary on your company pension and profit-sharing plans.
7) Decide in whose name you should own various assets:

- **Bank Accounts.** Establish a joint checking account while you maintain individual ones. This will make your budgeting easier. It will also give you more borrowing power.
- **Safety Deposit Box.** If you rent a safety deposit box, be aware that problems arise when married couples have joint ownership. There may be legal complications when one spouse dies. Contents of the box may be tied up if one spouse is sued by an outsider. One possible alternative: Each spouse owns a separate box with the other given power of attorney to act as agent.
- **Other Assets.** Ownership of a home, securities and other properties must be considered in light of tax and legal ramifications. The two principal forms of ownership for a husband and wife are single-party ownership by either spouse or some form of joint ownership.

8) Talk to employment benefits specialists and insurance agents about benefit changes if just one of you is working or about overlapping benefits if both of you are employed. Keep in mind that the value of your employment benefits might equal one-fourth or more of your combined salaries. If your salaries suddenly went up by 25 percent, you'd spend time in financial planning, so it makes sense to analyze your benefits, even though the money involved is not in cash. Some of the benefits you receive are fixed. But in at least three areas you have options:

- **Health Insurance.** Should you each retain your respective plan without dependent coverage or use just one that lists the other spouse as a dependent? *(See page 48.)*
- **Life Insurance.** Now that each of you will have a spouse, should you increase your coverage, with the other as beneficiary? If so,

would it be obtained more cheaply through your employer or bought on the outside? In analyzing your insurance needs, consider whether you should "ensure your insurability" by taking out your life insurance now. The point is that you may need to prove good health if you decide to buy it at a later date after you have children. (*See page 50.*)

- **Savings, Thrift, and Investment Plans.** If you and your spouse contribute to such plans and if you have to make choices among them, consider these factors: Which plans provide employer matching funds at a higher rate? Which offer more variety, such as investing in different stock and bond combinations instead of only in the company's own stock? Which have more flexibility, for example, more attractive loan and withdrawal privileges? Whose job is more stable, with longer-term employment prospects? You also should compare continued investments in these plans to investments in outside plans.

CONSIDER A PRENUPTIAL AGREEMENT

As you prepare for marriage, you may want to consider whether you should have a prenuptial agreement. This is a marriage contract that outlines the division of property in the event of divorce or death. It also may cover other matters, such as what happens if one of two working spouses is required to relocate. With over a million divorces occurring each year, many couples are using prenuptial agreements as a legal means of protecting themselves both financially and emotionally in the event a marriage breaks up.

Are you a good candidate for a prenuptial agreement? Think seriously about one if you answer "yes" to any of these questions: Were you married before? Are there children from a previous marriage? Is there a big difference in earnings and/or assets between you and your future mate or do you expect this to be the case in the future? Are you in line to receive a large inheritance or other windfall? Can you keep your emotions and finances separate?

Spouse Returns to Work. Usually the returning spouse is a woman. When that happens, the family and its finances are deeply affected. One positive result is another paycheck to help pay for expenses. There are also tax advantages:

- If you pay someone to care for children who are 14 or younger, you are entitled to a tax credit.
- When a husband and wife each earn income, they can deduct on their joint return 10 percent of the earned income of the lower-earning spouse up to $30,000 (maximum deduction $3,000). If the

lower-earning spouse makes any deductible contributions to an IRA or Keogh plan, you should reduce the spouse's earnings by that amount when you figure the 10 percent deduction.

But keep in mind that there are also financial disadvantages:

- You may have to spend some of the increased household income on work-related items such as meals, child care, and clothes.
- You will have less time to shop carefully and to prepare meals, so you may end up spending more on convenience foods.
- When two salaries are put together, there may be a significant jump in the couple's tax bracket.

Divorce. The financial problems that arise from a divorce are as numerous and difficult as the emotional ones.

To begin with, there are the legal fees. The cost of an uncontested divorce can be as low as $150—but rarely is. And if a divorce involves a court battle, legal fees may be $20,000 or more.

Then there is the matter of taxes. If you are paying alimony, the amount is tax deductible. If you receive alimony, you must report it as taxable income. Child support is not deductible and does not have to be reported. A transfer of appreciated property in settlement of marital rights is no longer considered a sale between the spouses, so no capital gains tax need be paid. However, if the property is later sold, the recipient of the property might then have to pay a substantial amount of capital gains tax on the proceeds of the sale.

Divorce affects the ownership of assets, from property of all kinds to pensions and Social Security. In many states, a couple can ask the court for an "equitable distribution" settlement if they cannot come to an agreement themselves. The distribution of assets in this no-fault divorce is based on contribution to the union.

In dividing up assets, the court will take note of such factors as the age and health of the couple, the duration of the marriage, the contribution each partner made to the career of the other, custody of any children, and loss of job potential. More and more, equitable distribution is replacing alimony in property settlements. In such a settlement, temporary alimony serves to support a dependent spouse until she or he can complete an education or get a job.

Remarriage—Blended Family. In a second marriage which involves former spouses and children, conflicts of financial interest are not unusual. A wife may want to take a long-desired vacation, but the husband's child from a prior marriage needs clothes for school. Child-care costs and alimony payments may cause discord. Such conflicts can threaten stability unless each partner understands and accepts the financial commitments of the other right at the start.

You may want to provide for your children from a previous marriage through specific bequests in your will. To do this, you can set up a trust that bequeaths income interest in property to a spouse without providing actual control over the property. The property goes to the children after the death of the spouse.

Life Experience: Home

If you decide to buy a home, which might be a house, a co-op, a condominium, or a mobile home, you should do so after comparing the pluses and minuses of owning and renting.

Renting. The principal advantages are: less out-of-pocket monthly costs; lack of concern about depreciating value and ongoing upkeep and maintenance; and greater flexibility—it's usually easier to rent a new apartment than to sell a house and buy a new one.

Owning. The principal advantages are: establishing psychological "roots;" realizing tax benefits (including deducting mortgage interest and property taxes); achieving "forced savings" to pay off the mortgage; and building up equity.

With equity, you can consider "trading up" by selling your old house and buying a costlier new one. Under current tax law, you will not have to pay capital gains tax if you buy a new home for more money within two years after selling your old one. And if you are over 55 and you sell your home at a profit, you can benefit from a one-time exemption from capital gains taxes (*see page 48*).

As a prospective buyer, your first move should be to determine how much you can afford to buy and maintain a house.

When you begin hunting for a home, you will of course be concerned with location, since it will affect both living conditions and the future value of the house. Consider such factors as the community—its government and economic stability; educational, religious, and medical facilities; property taxes and zoning laws; public transportation; police, firefighting, sanitation, water, sewage, and street lighting; environmental qualities such as noise and toxic fumes; shopping and banking; recreational, entertainment, and cultural opportunities; and city or town plans for the growth of the area.

Deficiencies in these factors may signal a neighborhood's decline. But the neighborhood may have declined in the past and be experiencing improvement now. Look for trends. Speak to residents and officials. Keep in mind that areas which appear to be on an upswing may not live up to their promise. The point is, the value of your home can depreciate as well as increase.

Before you buy a house, inspect every nook and cranny and order an engineer's report. Sometimes you can knock down the price if you find a serious problem. You can then remedy the problem by spending less than the difference in price. But beware—remedied defects can come back to haunt you.

Building. If you're building a home from your specifications, carefully select architects, builders, and contractors. As part of the selection process, get recommendations, conduct interviews, verify references, check with community organizations (Chamber of Commerce, Better Business Bureau), trade associations and dealers. Before giving out work, get competitive written bids on identical specifications.

Insist on a written contract which includes the specifications and cost. Be sure the contract details subcontractors, materials to be used, material suppliers, production and payment schedules, provisions for changes, and penalty clauses. Keep in mind that any time you deviate from architects' plans—even for minor adjustments—you will pay, perhaps dearly. Finally, plan to spend a great deal of time at the construction site to monitor progress.

If you're building from existing specifications, don't just go by the appearance of the model home you may have selected from among several models. Follow the procedures just described.

Financing. Few people pay cash in full to buy or build a home. Nearly all make a down payment and finance the rest through a mortgage. In most cases, the down payment will be at least 20 percent of the cost. The larger the down payment you make, of course, the lower your monthly mortgage payment will be, the smaller the overall interest you'll pay, and the faster you will build equity. Complete Worksheet 6, "Funding Your Home."

Mortgage. Your mortgage is likely to be one of the largest and most complicated credit arrangements of your lifetime. And your monthly mortgage payments are likely to be the biggest single expense in your budget. That's why it's so important to shop around carefully to compare lenders and mortgages. A slight difference in interest rates can make a significant difference in the overall amount of interest you'll have to pay over the life of the mortgage.

Check carefully for mortgage conditions not to your advantage, such as: penalties for prepaying your mortgage earlier than due or options allowing the lender to "call in" the loan early for cancellation or renewal at a higher interest rate because market conditions have changed.

Prospective sources for your mortgage include the seller, S&Ls, savings banks, commercial banks, credit unions, insurance compa-

Worksheet 6

FUNDING YOUR HOME

1. **AMOUNT NEEDED IN TODAY'S DOLLARS FOR DOWN PAYMENT AND OTHER COSTS:**	
a. Mortgage closing (down payment, origination fees, etc.) [based on 20% down payment on $100,000 home, plus fees]	$22,000
b. Closing costs such as title and legal fees	6,000
c. Moving costs	600
d. Partial payment on first year's property taxes, cost of new furnishings, miscellaneous expenses	5,000
e. Total amount needed in today's dollars	$33,600
2. **ADJUSTMENT FOR INFLATION:**	
a. How many years from now will you need this amount?	8
b. Estimate annual average rate of inflation between now and then	6%
c. Refer to Table A. Enter factor obtained by intersecting years and inflation %.	1.59
d. Multiply amount needed by factor 2.c. This gives you the amount needed *adjusted for inflation*	($33,600 x 1.59) $53,424
3. **ESTIMATED RETURN ON INVESTMENT:**	
a. Amount you currently have available in today's dollars.	$10,000
b. Estimate average annual rate of return on investment.	10%
c. Refer to Table A. Enter factor obtained by intersecting years 2.a. and % return on investment.	2.14
d. To calculate what your present funds will be worth through investment when you need them, multiply amount available by factor 3.c.	($10,000 x 2.14) $21,400
4. **SHORTAGE OR OVERAGE IN FUNDS YOU WILL NEED:** Subtract 3.d. from 2.d.	($53,424 – 21,400) $32,024
5. **IF OVERAGE:** Calculate lesser amount you must save/invest each year to accumulate inflation-adjusted amount 2.d.	
6. **IF SHORTAGE, ADDITIONAL INVESTMENT REQUIRED:**	
a. Refer to Table B. Enter factor obtained by intersecting years and estimated % return on investment 3.b.	11.4
b. Divide shortage 4. by factor 6.a.	($32,024 ÷ 11.4) $2,809

This is the additional amount (above funds currently available) that you must save/invest each year to accomplish your goal.

nies, mortgage bankers, private lenders, real estate investment trusts, and the Farmers Home Administration Office (FmHA) (which serves people living in rural areas who have moderate and low incomes). The Federal Housing Administration (FHA) and the Veterans Administration (VA) insure lenders against loss on mortgages available to qualified applicants. Private mortgage insurance (PMI) is also available. You can reduce your down payments to as little as 5 percent if you can get a commercial insurance company to insure your mortgage. Of course, you pay for this insurance.

There are various ways to finance through the seller:

Assumable Mortgage. You take over the balance of the seller's mortgage (this happens less and less frequently). Among other possible benefits, when you arrange an assumable mortgage you don't have to pay any loan origination fee, a cost that can be substantial.

Purchase Money Mortgage. The seller grants you a loan for the purchase price less your down payment.

Seller's Second Mortgage. This combines an existing mortgage assumption with a purchase money mortgage. You assume the existing mortgage. This mortgage doesn't cover the entire purchase price minus the down payment, so you also obtain a new loan from the seller to cover the balance.

Types of mortgages available from other lending sources include:

- **Fixed Rate.** Your monthly payments remain the same throughout the life of the mortgage.
- **Graduated Payments.** A mortgage designed primarily for young, first-time owners whose rising income over the years will keep pace with mortgage payments that increase from an unusually low initial level.
- **Adjustable (or Flexible) Rate (ARM).** The interest rate on this mortgage is changed at predetermined periods to reflect fluctuations in a financial index agreed to by you and the lender.
- **Balloon Payment.** This mortgage provides low monthly payments, typically interest only, for a relatively few years. The buyer then pays off the balance all at once.

Based on these and other mortgage arrangements, a wide range of financing possibilities can be designed to accommodate most buyers' needs. Bankers and real estate brokers can be consulted for their creative financing ideas. Be cautious, however. Consider all the "what if" possibilities before coming to a decision.

At the closing—when title changes hands from the seller to you—be sure your lawyer is present, that you have your mortgage, and that you obtain all the documents needed from the seller and are supplied with all the documents required by state and local authorities.

You must be prepared to pay for closing costs. These may total 6 to 7 percent of the purchase price and include fees relating to legal counsel, title, and the mortgage. You will also face other expenses such as homeowner's insurance, moving, and the cost of new furnishings.

Home Equity Loans. Equity is the difference between what you owe on your mortgage and the amount of net proceeds if you sell your home. Equity on a home is the largest single asset held by most people. This equity grows with every mortgage payment and usually with inflation. But it's not liquid. It earns no income and doesn't pay your bills or improve your standard of living. It can, however, be used as the basis for a loan. Such a loan generally takes two forms:

- **Amortized Second Mortgages.** You receive all the loan funds in one lump sum. Normally you pay a fixed interest rate over a predetermined repayment period. These loans carry higher interest rates and shorter repayment schedules than first mortgages.
- **Line of Credit or Cash Reserves.** Once you've established either a credit line or cash reserves, you can borrow against it and repay at will, just as you do with a bank credit card. You pay interest only on the money in use. Usually you pay floating interest rates set periodically and pegged to some agreed-upon financial benchmark—such as one or two percent over the prevailing prime rate or market price of U.S. Treasury bills. There are few, if any, strings on how you use home equity loans. They're usually granted on the basis of your home's market value and your ability to repay.

Before taking such a loan, consider the negatives:

- It is linked to a lien on your house—that is, your house is the collateral, and you can lose it if you fail to repay the loan.
- It reduces the future borrowing power on your house.
- It may encourage you to spend or use funds excessively—as many people have found themselves doing with credit cards.

For further discussion of home financing, see Sylvia Porter's Personal Finance Guide, *Buying and Selling a Home*.

Life Experience: Children

Financial planning is a vital priority for couples who are deciding whether to have children. The planning will, of course, be focused on the expense. The couples' financial situation might affect their decision to have a child now, to wait, or to have fewer children.

Rising Costs. The initial costs of giving birth—including the hospital and routine delivery—may run around $2,500. Most health/major medical insurance policies cover a large portion of this. Subsequent costs include clothes, special care, food, medical, recreation, and the like. There are also indirect expenses, such as a bigger house, higher utility bills, higher insurance costs, and more. And family income may be diminished if one parent has to leave work to take care of children. Beyond that, the costs increase substantially in the teen years. Expenses are about 200 percent higher when children reach the age of 18 than in the birth year.

Financial Moves. With the birth of each child you must adjust your financial planning. This means rebudgeting. First refigure Worksheet 1 (income, expenses, net cash flow). You will be adding each baby to your health/major medical insurance; you will need to re-evaluate your disability income (*see Worksheet 10*) and life insurance needs (*see Worksheet 12*). And you will need to revise your will.

Your Children Go to College. Paying for your children's college educations is a big financial commitment. Total costs at private colleges may range from $4,000 to $14,000 or more a year. If you begin to put money away when a child is a youngster and continue to do so regularly over the years, you will make one of your best "investments." To plan your investment program for college educations, complete Worksheet 7, "Funding a College Education."

One way to accumulate funds for a child's college education is to put money into a special savings account or into a money market account for the child with you as the custodian under the Uniform Gifts to Minors Act. (In the latter case, you will need to make a substantial minimum deposit.) Setting these funds aside reinforces your commitment to this objective. In addition, you may avoid taxes on the interest because the child has a low tax bracket or pays no taxes at all. You should investigate the laws in your state that govern how such funds can be dispensed, since this may affect the tax status.

TIPS ON GETTING FINANCIAL AID

If you cannot accumulate enough money through what you save and invest, together with what children may earn working part-time and summers, you may be able to obtain financial aid for college or vocational education after high school. The main sources of this aid are the federal and state governments, the school, and community or private groups. Aid is available in four basic forms:

FUNDING A COLLEGE EDUCATION

Note: A separate worksheet for the college education of the Smiths' second child resulted in a savings/investment goal of $309 per year over 20 years (see Worksheet 13).

Worksheet 7

FUNDING A COLLEGE EDUCATION

(Complete a separate worksheet for each child.)

1. **AMOUNT NEEDED IN TODAY'S DOLLARS FOR FOUR-YEAR PRIVATE COLLEGE* EDUCATION:**
   a. Total education costs (tuition, books, equipment, supplies, school fees, etc.) $18,000
   b. Living expenses while at school (room and board, clothing, recreation, etc.) 14,000
   c. Total 32,000
   d. Subtract estimated funds available from loans, grants, scholarships, other outside sources 16,000
   e. Amount of your own contribution in today's dollars. 16,000

2. **ADJUSTMENT FOR INFLATION:**
   a. How many years from now will you need this amount? 14
   b. Estimate average annual rate of inflation between now and then. 6%
   c. Refer to Table A. Enter factor obtained by intersecting years and inflation %. 2.26
   d. Multiply amount needed by factor 2.c. This gives you the amount needed *adjusted for inflation*. .... ($16,000 × 2.26) $36,160

3. **ESTIMATED RETURN ON INVESTMENT:**
   a. Amount you currently have available in today's dollars. $5,000
   b. Estimate average annual return on investment. 10%
   c. Refer to Table A. Enter factor obtained by intersecting years 2.a. by % return on investment. 3.80
   d. To calculate what your present funds will be worth through investment when you need them, multiply amount available 3.a. by factor 3.c. .... ($5,000 × 3.80) $19,000

4. **SHORTAGE OR OVERAGE IN FUNDS YOU WILL NEED:**
   Subtract 3.d. from 2.d. .... ($36,160 − 19,000) $17,160

5. **IF OVERAGE:**
   Calculate lesser amount you must save/invest each year to accumulate inflation-adjusted amount 2.d. .... ______

6. **IF SHORTAGE, ADDITIONAL INVESTMENT REQUIRED:**
   a. Refer to Table B. Enter factor obtained by intersecting years and estimated % return on investment 3.b. 28.0
   b. Divide shortage in 4. by factor 6.a. .... ($17,160 ÷ 28) $612

This is the additional amount (above funds currently available) that you must save/invest each year to accomplish your goal.

*Other educational options will of course result in different funding estimates.

1) **Grants.** These are based on the student's or family's need and do not have to be repaid.
2) **Scholarships.** These are based on talent, ability, or need, and do not have to be repaid.
3) **Student Work/Study Programs.** These enable a student to earn money at work that is tied in with study programs.
4) **Loans.** These vary in interest rates and starting dates for repayment depending on the source of the loan and the program.

Urge your child to try first to get grants and scholarships. Ask every school that your child applies to for complete information on expected expenses and on financial aid. Find out if the school participates in federal and/or any other aid programs. For current information on federal programs, including loans, call the Student Information Center (301) 984-4070. For information on state assistance, call your state's department of education.

Tap private sources of grants and scholarships, too, even though this money is harder to get. Start with the schools themselves. In doing this, college-bound students and parents should consult with high school guidance counselors and college financial aid advisers. Keep in mind that need is not based on family income alone, but on the difference between how much a family can afford to pay and what it costs to attend the school.

Other sources of scholarships are foundations, labor unions, trade associations, professional groups, and special interest, fraternal, minority, and civic and cultural community service organizations. Your company may also award scholarships to children of employees. And your child might be eligible for one of the 5,000 scholarships offered by the National Merit Scholarship Corporation. These are awarded on the basis of scores on the Preliminary Scholastic Aptitude Test/National Merit Scholarship Qualifying Test (PSAT/NMSQT).

Loans are the last resort—but the one available to the greatest number of people. The federal government generally offers the best rates and terms. But federal loans are limited and frequently prospective borrowers must turn to private lending institutions. (See Sylvia Porter's Personal Finance Guide, *Financing Higher Education.)*

Your Last Child Leaves Home. A number of changes take place in your finances when your last child is on his or her own.

- Your expenses will be reduced, but this reduction will be lessened somewhat because you'll pay more in taxes when you declare fewer dependents.
- You will need less cash reserves for emergencies.
- A homemaker spouse may decide to return to work.

- You may increase your expenses by improving your lifestyle. But you still will probably have enough left over for additional investing. With your expenses and obligations cut back, you might want to become more aggressive in your investing *(see page 20)*.

Consider also what may be your largest investment to date—the home you own. With your children gone, your house may be too large for you and selling it might be wise. If you bought a smaller home or rented, the funds available could also be invested.

After each child marries, you may again want to make revisions in your estate planning and your will—especially if the newlyweds have children. You might want to make provisions for your grandchildren in your will. *(See Life Experience: Estate Planning, page 52.)*

Life Experience: Upgrading Your Lifestyle

Your standard of living is shaped partially by what you can afford and partially by what you prefer.

Major lifestyle expenses must be considered in terms of both cost and preference. If you had to choose, would you prefer: a smaller home with amenities or a larger home without them? Such amenities as fireplaces, modern kitchens, and master bedroom suites with luxury baths are becoming standard in many new smaller homes. But of course their cost is reflected in the price of the house.

When you have narrowed down your choices on the basis of what you'd prefer, you are ready to consider whether to make them goals. You are then faced with the question of what you can afford. An obvious consideration is whether a potential goal is to be realized on a shorter- or longer-term basis.

To evaluate your capacity to finance a prospective goal, complete Worksheet 8, "Funding a Large Lifestyle Expenditure." It will tell you approximately what amount you must save or invest over what number of years in order to make your goal a reality. But keep in mind that your lifestyle choices may conflict with other elements of your financial planning program. Such conflicts will be resolved when you complete Worksheet 13, "Putting It All Together."

Life Experience: Adversities

Many of life's painful reversals can't be predicted. But you can take measures to protect yourself, your family, and your assets against possible future calamities such as major medical expenses, prolonged disability, losing your job, and having to care for aging parents.

Health Insurance. Health insurance offers vital protection, and you should be sure that you have enough. Begin this evaluation by completing Worksheet 9, "Do You Have Enough Health Insurance?"

Worksheet 8

FUNDING A LARGE LIFESTYLE EXPENDITURE

(Complete a separate worksheet for each expenditure)

1. **AMOUNT NEEDED IN TODAY'S DOLLARS FOR A LARGE LIFESTYLE EXPENDITURE:**	(Automobile)
a. Estimated cost of purchase.	$12,000
b. Cost of purchase to be borrowed, such as through installment payments.	9,600
c. Amount of your own contribution in today's dollars.	2,400
2. **ADJUSTMENT FOR INFLATION:**	
a. How many years from now will you need this amount?	3
b. Estimate average annual rate of inflation between now and then.	6%
c. Refer to Table A. Enter factor obtained by intersecting years and inflation %.	1.19
d. Multiply amount of your own funds 1.c. by factor 2.c. This gives you the amount needed *adjusted for inflation*.	($2,400 × 1.19) $2,856
3. **ESTIMATED RETURN ON INVESTMENT:**	
a. Amount you currently have available in today's dollars.	$1,000
b. Estimate average annual return on investment.	8%
c. Refer to Table A. Enter factor obtained by intersecting years 2.a. and % return on investment 3.b.	1.26
d. To find out what your present funds will be worth through investment when you need them, multiply amount available 3.a. by factor 3.c.	($1,000 × 1.26) $1,260
4. **SHORTAGE OR OVERAGE IN FUNDS YOU WILL NEED:** Subtract 3.d. from 2.d.	($2,856 − 1,260) $1,596
5. **IF OVERAGE:** Calculate lesser amount you must save/invest to accumulate inflation-adjusted amount 2.d.	
6. **IF SHORTAGE, ADDITIONAL INVESTMENT REQUIRED:**	
a. Refer to Table B. Enter factor obtained by intersecting years and estimated % return on investment 3.b.	3.3
b. Divide the shortage in 4. by factor 6.a.	($1,596 ÷ 3.3) $484

This is the additional amount (above funds currently available) that you must save/invest each year to accomplish your goal.

Your evaluation should take note of these considerations:

- Group health insurance obtained through employers, labor unions and other groups usually costs considerably less than individual coverage.
- You might want to supplement group policies with individual policies to be fully protected. Examine your policies carefully to determine what health conditions and medical services are excluded; at what age benefits for your children or you and your spouse will be terminated; and under what circumstances policies can be cancelled or not renewed by the insurer.

Disability Income Insurance. You probably know how much life insurance you have. But do you know how much disability income insurance you have? Most people don't. Yet, if you are under age 65, the odds are far greater that you'll suffer a disability serious enough to keep you away from work for more than three months than that you will die. To see how you would fare if this eventuality occurred, complete Worksheet 10, "Disability Income."

Consider these factors:

- Coverage should be "noncancellable." Note also that "guaranteed renewable" coverage must be renewed by the insurer—but *not necessarily at the same premium rate*.
- If disability is defined as "inability to engage in any occupation," you're allowed to collect benefits only if you can't work at all. Significantly better is "inability to engage in your own occupation." You could then engage in another form of work and still collect full or partial benefits.
- Note the treatment of the extent of your incapacity to work. Will you experience loss of income benefits if you are able to work but only on a reduced schedule?
- Does a period of total disability have to precede a period of partial disability before benefits are paid—for instance, a massive stroke that then necessitated a reduced work day? If so, what happens if you have a deteriorating condition such as multiple sclerosis? Would you be covered if you could not work a five-day week? (See Sylvia Porter's Personal Finance Guide, *Buying Insurance*.)

Economic Reversals. As was noted earlier, your financial planning should begin with the provision of a cash cushion against a sudden economic reversal. This cash reserve should be large enough to tide you over for three to six months. You should also establish a good credit rating and the borrowing power to take care of contingencies your cash reserves will not cover.

(Continued on page 46)

Worksheet 9

DO YOU HAVE ENOUGH HEALTH INSURANCE?

HEALTH CARE	1. Estimated Average Current Costs in Your Locale	2. Approximate Benefits Provided by Your Current Coverage* (in dollars or % of column 1)	3. Approximate Additional Benefits Coverage You May Need (in dollars or % of column 1)
IN HOSPITAL:			
Room and board (daily)	______	______	______
Intensive care (daily)	______	______	______
Special nurses (per shift)	______	______	______
Drugs (estimated)	______	______	______
Medical supplies and appliances (estimated)	______	______	______
Radiology (list types)	______	______	______
Laboratory tests (list types)	______	______	______
Surgical (per types of operations):			
Surgeon	______	______	______
Anesthesia	______	______	______
Operating room	______	______	______
Physician (visiting)	______	______	______
Maternity (doctor, etc.)	______	______	______
OTHER FACILITIES:			
Ambulatory	______	______	______
Psychiatric	______	______	______
Alcohol and Drug	______	______	______
Emergency	______	______	______
Convalescent/Rehabilitation	______	______	______
Nursing	______	______	______
OTHER SERVICES:			
Ambulances	______	______	______
Other medical transport	______	______	______
Home care (list drugs, supplies, appliances and services)	______	______	______
Dental (list services)	______	______	______
Psychiatric (list services)	______	______	______
Physiotherapy (list services)	______	______	______
OTHER EXPENSES:	______	______	______

*Estimate maximum number of days

Fill out this chart to see if your health insurance coverage is adequate. Keep in mind that, in addition to adequate health insurance coverage, you require disability income coverage for your regular living expenses, as a replacement for lost earnings (*see Worksheet 10*).

Worksheet 10

DISABILITY INCOME

1. MONTHLY AVERAGE OF TOTAL LIVING EXPENSES WHILE DISABLED (PER WORKSHEET 1) ($22,815 ÷ 12) $ 901

This amount should be adjusted as follows:

a. Increased because of related unreimbursed health care expenses. ______

b. Reduced because of waivers of premium clauses on health and life insurance during period of disablement (check policies). ______

TOTAL ______

2. MONTHLY AVERAGE OF SUBSTITUTE INCOME WHILE DISABLED THROUGH ILLNESS OR INJURY	Monthly Benefits		
	Immediate*	After 6 Months	After 2 Years**
Group Disability Insurance (Tax-free if you have paid premiums; taxable with an annual exemption of $5,200 if you haven't.)	✓	✓	✓
Social Security (Benefits begin with sixth month. Dependents also qualify for certain benefits. Consult Social Security Office.)	______	$893	______
State Disability Plans	✓	✓	✓
Workers' Compensation	✓	✓	✓
Veterans Administration	✓	✓	✓
Personal Disability Insurance (Tax-free)	✓	✓	✓
Spouse's Income	______	______	______
Savings and Investment Income (Interest, dividends, rents, etc.)	($2,100 ÷ 12) $175	______	______
Legal Settlements Because of Disabling Accident	______	______	______
Funds Set Aside toward Financial Goals (per other worksheets)	______	______	______
TOTAL MONTHLY SUBSTITUTE INCOME	______	______	______
3. SHORTAGE OR OVERAGE (EXPENSES LESS INCOME)	______	______	______
4. BORROWING POWER (Using borrowed or withdrawn funds from life insurance, employee pension, savings, etc.)	______	______	______
5. ADDITIONAL DISABILITY INCOME COVERAGE NEEDED (Item 3 minus Item 4)	______	______	______

*Waiting period may be up to or more than 90 days.

**You may want to consider effect of inflation on your needs (Use Table A).

✓ = Check with appropriate issuer of insurance.

If an unforeseen event plunges you and your previously sound credit rating into chaos, pare your budget. If your finances really are out of control, seek credit counseling (often available without charge from local government agencies) to help you set up a new budget and create an extended repayment plan with your creditors.

The absolute last-ditch alternative is to declare bankruptcy. You can't be punished for choosing this option—for example, you can't lose your job. Bankruptcy provides you with a fresh start, but it stays on your credit record for 10 years and can hamper your financial recovery during that time.

Caring for Aging Parents. Aiding aging parents, financially and physically, can pose problems. Your elderly parents' financial needs may have a serious impact on your own. But caring for elderly parents is a responsibility that most children are willing to assume. Your aim should be to minimize the pressure put on both you and your parents.

You may find that sharing your home with your parents not only eliminates the cost of long-distance or institutionalized care, but also creates a rewarding extended family situation. But it doesn't work for everyone. Often power and personality conflicts prevent two or three generations from living under the same roof. In these cases, you may want to consult agencies that match up elderly roommates or bring together an elderly person or elderly couple and a young couple who would like an extended family. You may be able to find suitable housing for your parents in apartment buildings specifically designed for the elderly or in a variety of senior-citizen communities.

If a parent is too ill for these options or if you cannot have your parent with you, consider these alternatives:

- **Home-Care Program.** There are many home-care programs which include meals and medical services for older adults. Home care may have a prohibitive price tag if your parent needs intensive medical attention. The bills for at-home, around-the-clock care may cost $50,000 or more annually.

  Medicare, the federal health insurance program for the elderly and disabled, will pay for most home health care visits if skilled medical or nursing care is required. But Medicare will not pay for general household services or custodial care that an elderly person might need.

  The Medicaid program pays medical costs for those financially unable to pay these costs themselves. To qualify for Medicaid, patients are expected to use up most of their monetary resources before they become eligible for assistance. A controversial legal loophole that elderly parents have used to avoid this is to set up a trust that transfers property to a child, thus protecting those assets from being called upon to pay medical bills. The parent can have power over the assets and income up until the time he or she is incapacitated. The trust must be set up at least two years prior to the onset of illness or Medicaid will not provide assistance.

- **Nursing Home.** When at-home care is not feasible for a variety of medical and financial reasons, a nursing home may be an alternative. Not that nursing homes are inexpensive—costs can average $1,250 to $3,000 a month.

  Select with care is the cardinal rule for choosing a nursing home. It's wise to arrive without an appointment so that you can be certain there's no "staging" done before your inspection. Determine whether the nursing home has received Medicare and Medicaid certification. These programs have set standards for services, safety, and sanitation; they also may be able to help you cover the costs. Also check on fire safety and cleanliness, staff credentials, and facilities such as activity rooms. Before you sign a contract, have an attorney look at it. Some homes reserve the right to discharge a patient whose condition has deteriorated—even if a nonrefundable lump-sum payment was made.

Keep in mind that if your parent is a dependent, you can deduct on your taxes payments for nursing and medical treatment (but not room and board).

You can obtain lists of accredited nursing homes from the American Association of Homes for the Aging, 1050 17th St., N.W., Washington, DC 20036; the American Health Care Association, 1200 15th St., N.W., Washington, DC 20005; and the National Council of Health Centers, 2600 Virginia Ave., N.W., Suite 1100, Washington, DC 20037.

Life Experience: Retirement

There are good reasons why you should begin to make a success of old age when you are young. If you rely on Social Security as your sole financial support in retirement, your standard of living will decline. You should think of Social Security as supplemental income for retirement, not its financial foundation. Even if you earn enough each year over your career to qualify you for the maximum Social Security payment, when you retire at age 65 your monthly check will probably be considerably less than you have been accustomed to living on. It is unlikely that payments from your pension will make up the difference. The average monthly pension payment is currently estimated to be about $330.

Investment. Your goal must be to establish a solid financial base that will maintain your standard of living in retirement. During your working days, you should participate to the greatest extent possible in tax-favored, employment-oriented investment plans such as IRAs, Keoghs, profit-sharing, tax-deferred, and pensions. Over the years, you should invest for capital growth in these plans (where choice is possible) and do the same in your other investments. Your aim is twofold: to exceed the effects of inflation and to build up the principal you can convert to higher income-paying investments as you near and then enter your retirement. (Fill out Worksheet 11, "Funding Your Retirement.")

Tax strategies are very important to your investment planning. You may be able to take lump-sum distributions from employment plans and use the 10-year forward averaging formula to reduce your taxes. Or you may be able to roll these distributions into IRA investments that are tax-sheltered.

You should not be too conservative in your investments. Typically, retired couples do not give adequate consideration to the effects of even moderate inflation on their relatively fixed retirement income.

Here are some other factors to take into consideration:

Home. Will you want to sell it and buy something smaller, rent, or move to a different area? The sale of your home can provide a big boost in disposable and investment funds. If you are over age 55, retired, and have lived in your house for three of the past five years, you may realize tax benefits on any gain from the sale.

Life Insurance Policies. Many retirees find they no longer need all of their life insurance coverage, since they no longer have young families to protect and/or have made other provisions for relatives in the event of death. Life insurance policies can be changed, cashed in, or drawn upon for additional retirement income. Your estate planning will affect your decisions. (See Worksheet 12, "How Much Life Insurance Do You Need?")

Health Insurance Coverage. Good health insurance coverage is one of the best ways to protect all your other assets. If you or your spouse is struck by a prolonged illness and you don't have proper coverage, you could find all your resources drained by the payment of medical bills. And, of course, as people get older they're more likely to be sick more often. (Check Worksheet 9, "Do You Have Enough Health Insurance?")

When you are about to retire, find out if you can convert the group insurance coverage you have through your company to an individual plan. Medicare starts paying medical bills after you're 65, but it

Worksheet 11

FUNDING YOUR RETIREMENT

1. **DESIRED ANNUAL RETIREMENT INCOME IN TODAY'S DOLLARS:**	$18,000
2. **ADJUSTMENT FOR INFLATION:**	
a. How many years from now will your retirement commence?....................................	30
b. Estimate average annual rate of inflation between now and then....................................	6%
c. Refer to Table A. Enter factor obtained by intersecting years and inflation %.	5.74
d. Multiply projected annual income by factor 2.c. This will give you the amount of annual income you'll need *adjusted for inflation*.	($18,000 × 5.74) $103,320
3. **ESTIMATED INCOME FROM CURRENT SOURCES:**	
a. Annual income you now project from Social Security, employment and other group retirement plans, IRAs, Keoghs, interest, dividends, rents and any other sources—in today's dollars.......................	$12,000
b. Estimate average annual return on rate of growth in amount 3.a. (Note: Rate of growth in Social Security is based on cost of living adjustment.)	6%
c. Refer to Table A. Enter factor obtained by intersecting years 2.a. and % return on investment...	5.74
d. To calculate the increased value of your projected annual income when you will need it, multiply 3.a. by factor 3.c.....................................	($12,000 × 5.74) $68,880
4. **SHORTAGE OR OVERAGE IN ANNUAL INCOME:** Subtract 3.d. from 2.d.	$33,440
5. **IF SHORTAGE, ADDITIONAL INVESTMENT REQUIRED:**	
a. Now you must determine how much additional capital you must have *when you retire* to produce the additional amount of annual income indicated in 4. To calculate this, divide 4. by your estimate of the % return on investment you will realize over the years between now and your retirement. .... This is the additional amount of money you will need to accumulate between now and your retirement to produce the additional amount of annual retirement income indicated in 4.	($33,440 ÷ .08 [8%]) $418,000
b. Refer to Table B. Enter factor obtained by intersecting years and estimated % return on amount 5.a..................................	113.1
c. Divide 5.a by factor 5.b.	($418,000 ÷ 113.1) $3,696

This is the additional amount that you must save/invest each year over and above current projected income, Item 3.a., to produce the annual retirement income you want.

Worksheet 12

HOW MUCH LIFE INSURANCE DO YOU NEED?

(Filled in for Mr. Smith)

Whom do you want to protect with your life insurance? ☒ Spouse ☒ Children
☐ Children from a prior marriage ☐ Parents Other ________

To what extent do you want to protect them? ☒ Provide for their present lifestyle
☐ More affluent lifestyle ☐ More modest lifestyle

How long do you want to protect each? Until children finish college

For simplicity, assume that increases in beneficiaries' income will keep pace with increases from inflation.

I. LUMP-SUM BENEFITS AND EXPENSES WHEN YOU DIE

A. Lump-Sum Benefits	
1. From your present individual insurances.	$75,000
2. From your present employment and other group insurances.	25,000
3. Death benefits from your pension, profit sharing, deferred income, and other plans.	
4. From Social Security, veterans', and other government sources	255
5. Other: ________	
6. Total Lump-Sum Benefits	100,255
B. Lump-Sum Expenses	
1. Cemetery plot and funeral costs (not prepaid).	2,000
2. Non-health-insured costs of an expensive terminal illness.	
3. Tax, probate, attorney, and other state expenses.	300
4. To pay your existing debts not collateralized, or covered by redemption insurance.	
5. Transitional funds to help tide your beneficiaries over as they adjust after your death.	
6. Other: ________	
7. Total Lump-Sum Expenses	2,300
C. Difference Between Benefits and Expenses Above	
1. Excess of benefits over expenses.	$97,955
2. Excess of expenses over benefits.	

doesn't pay all the bills. Nor does Medicaid. Make sure your private policy or policies will pay all or part of what Medicare misses. Senior citizen health and life insurance policies are available from various private companies and associations (such as the American Association of Retired Persons, 1909 K St., N.W., Washington, DC 20049).

Other Retirement Strategies. You may want to hold a part-time job or start a part-time business after you retire, to bring in additional

HOW MUCH LIFE INSURANCE DO YOU NEED?

II. INCOME AND EXPENSES AFTER YOUR DEATH OF THOSE TO BE PROTECTED

A. Annual Income	
1. Net working income (after taxes and pay deductions).	
2. Income from interest, dividends, rents, etc. from assets owned by survivors (some of which may have been inherited from you).	2,100
3. Income from your individual, employment, government, and other insurances and programs (above) that pay in installments rather than lump sums.	12,000
4. Interest, dividends, or other income from investment of the amount left over, if any, I.C above.	5,900
5. Other ______	
6. Total Income	20,000
B. Annual Expenses	
1. Ordinary living expenses (food, housing, clothing, transportation, insurance, recreation, etc.).	17,000
2. Extraordinary expenses, if any, survivors may incur (such as college educations and weddings).	1,000
3. Total Expenses	$18,000
C. Difference Between Income and Expenses	
1. Amount of income exceeding expenses.	$ 2,000
2. Amount of expenses exceeding income.	

III. DO YOU NEED MORE LIFE INSURANCE, OR ARE YOU OVERINSURED?

A. If you have an excess of expenses over benefits in Item I.C.2, you will need additional life insurance providing lump-sum proceeds.	
B. If your beneficiaries will lack income to cover their expense as revealed in Item II.C.2, you will need more life insurance to provide this income. The income will be paid either by the policies or will be generated from the return on investment of lump sums paid by the policies. (Calculate lump sum needed by estimating after-tax return on investment that will provide missing income in II.C.2.)	

Note 1: Items II.C.1., II.C.2, and III.B. should be adjusted to provide for terminating payment to some beneficiaries at a given time, such as when children grow up.

Note 2: You may be paying for more insurance than you need if you end up with ongoing income that substantially exceeds ongoing expenses in Item II.C.1.

income and to remain productive. Depending on your age, you can earn various amounts and not lose any Social Security benefits. At age 70, you can earn any amount and still receive full benefits.

Then again, retirement at any age may be wrong for you. Some companies encourage employees to continue working beyond retirement age, if only part-time. (See Sylvia Porter's Personal Finance Guide, *Planning for Retirement.*)

Life Experience: Estate Planning

Planning for your death is not a particularly pleasant task. But it is vitally necessary and one of the most helpful and caring things you can do for your family. Complete Worksheet 12, ''How Much Life Insurance Do You Need?'' which covers such matters as benefits, life insurance, beneficiaries, income and expenses, and burial expenses.

Here are some aspects of estate planning needing special attention:

Preparing a Will. A will is essential. Without it, the state will control how your property is distributed. This places your family in a difficult and perhaps divisive situation. The purpose of your will is to provide for and protect those people you care about—your beneficiaries. Be sure it:

- Presents clear instructions for distributing assets.
- Assures that your assets will be properly managed.
- Provides for reasonable continuation of your family's lifestyle.
- Reduces or eliminates the tax burden of your heirs.

If you are married, you and your spouse should both draw up wills.

Certain life experiences will trigger the need to update your will(s). Among these are the death of a beneficiary, executor or trustee; the birth of a child; divorce; and substantial changes in your assets. If periodic review produces relatively few changes, you may be able to update your existing will by adding a codicil to it.

Safe Deposit Box. Do not put the original of your will in your safe deposit box. It should be kept with your attorney or executor. A copy can be kept in your box. Similarly, put in your box copies, not the originals, of your life insurance policies. Many states have regulations prohibiting spouses from removing property from a safe deposit box. Life insurance is considered property. Should the estate become tied up in probate courts, there is no way an insurance company can pay the beneficiary, since a death certificate *and* the insurance policy are required for payment.

Here are some other documents you should put in your box: birth certificates; important legal papers; military discharge papers; divorce decrees; marriage licenses; and other significant personal papers. Also include a detailed inventory of all household furnishings, indicating costs and, ideally, providing photos. Include as well property records, such as mortgages; insurance policies—homeowners, auto, health, and others except life; and securities of all kinds. For ready reference, make photocopies of the papers in your box to keep at home. (See Sylvia Porter's Personal Finance Guide, *Estate Planning.*)

IV. Putting It All Together

Formulating a Final Plan. Now that you have gone through the process of financial planning as it applies to the varying life experiences you may undergo, you are ready to formulate a final plan that realistically allocates the amounts you must save and invest each year to realize your financial goals.

Look at Worksheet 13, "Putting It All Together." To complete this worksheet you will have to refer to the worksheets you completed for the goals listed beneath "Five Financial Goals," a home, college education, lifestyle expenditure, your own business, retirement. One or more of these may not be applicable to your combined financial planning. You may have decided, for example, not to buy a house, or not to fund your own business. For the goals that are applicable to you, refer to the relevant worksheets you've already completed. On Worksheet 13, enter in the column beneath each goal the annual amount you have determined you will need in order to achieve that goal and fill in that amount for the necessary number of years.

Then fill in the right-hand column, "Totals for Each Year," by adding the figures across the worksheet. In the same way, add the columns from top to bottom to arrive at totals. Your grand total should be the same for the horizontal and vertical addition you've done.

Analyzing the Worksheet. Now analyze what the worksheet means. The essential point for your financial well-being is that *your totals for each year must not exceed your annual capacity to save and/or invest that amount.*

If the totals are higher than that capacity, you need to go back and redo the worksheets involved, revising your planning so that you arrive at a realistic figure.

You might want to consider these options:

- Increase your income by revising your investment objectives or by seeking additional employment income.
- Reduce your variable expenses.
- Rank your objectives and eliminate the least important.
- Decrease the costs of your objectives (such as a less expensive college education or home).
- Start some of your goals later (for example, postpone a large lifestyle expenditure).

In this way, you will be able to put together a financial plan of action that works for you. Once you have done that, you have fulfilled the goal of financial planning.

HOW TO USE THIS WORKSHEET

1. Under "Years" column, enter years for the maximum number of years you entered on Worksheets 5, 6, 7, 8, and 11.
2. Under "Financial Objectives," enter the dollar amount shown on these worksheets as "Additional Investment Required." This is the amount you must save/invest each year above funds presently available to accomplish your financial goals. Use a separate column to accommodate each goal for which you prepared a worksheet, i.e., two columns for two college educations.
3. Add totals. Totals should coincide across bottom and down right-hand column.
4. Note that the totals for financial goals (vertical columns) are less than the amounts recorded as Item 4. on the worksheets. The reason is that the column totals do not reflect the growth produced by savings/investment at given rates of interest.

Worksheet 13

PUTTING IT ALL TOGETHER	
Financial Objectives	
YEARS	Business
Year 1:1985	$1,025
Year 2:1986	1,025
Year 3:1987	1,025
Year 4:1988	1,025
Year 5:1989	1,025
Year 6:1990	
Year 7:1991	
Year 8:1992	
Year 9:1993	
Year 10:1994	
Year 11:1995	
Year 12:1996	
Year 13:1997	
Year 14:1998	
Year 15:1999	
Year 16:2000	
Year 17:2001	
Year 18:2002	
Year 19:2003	
Year 20:2004	
Year 21:2005	
Year 22:2006	
Year 23:2007	
Year 24:2008	
Year 25:2009	
Year 26:2010	
Year 27:2011	
Year 28:2012	
Year 29:2013	
Year 30:2014	
TOTALS	$5,125

PUTTING IT ALL TOGETHER

When the "Smith Family" completed Worksheet 13, "Putting It All Together," they discovered that they would have to save/invest more than they had anticipated each year to accomplish the financial objectives they had previously arrived at in Worksheets 5, 6, 7, 8, and 11.

This may well be the case with many readers. It points up the fact that accomplishing an integrated set of financial goals is not easy and requires very careful planning.

Mr. and Mrs. Smith did not want to eliminate any of their financial objectives. At the same time, they were unable to reduce their current expenses in any significant measure.

Adjustments after Completing Worksheets

How did the Smiths adjust the worksheet results to the reality of their financial situation?

1. They discussed ways to increase their income. Mr. Smith would look for a better-paying job. He would also consider "moonlighting" in a second job. Mrs. Smith would proceed with her plan to start her own business.
2. They would redouble their efforts to obtain an increased rate of return on their savings/investments. Over the long run, even small increments of increase would help substantially in achieving their goals.
3. They would consider having their two children attend public colleges instead of private ones. This would reduce their education costs in today's uninflated dollars by about $3,200 a year over four years for each of the children.
4. They might buy/build a less costly home than the $100,000 one they had planned on. They also might consider acquiring a two-family home so that they could rent the extra unit and achieve tax benefits.
5. They would reduce their current contribution to their retirement plan and then increase it after their children left home and they had more disposable income. They would also establish a Keogh plan when Mrs. Smith began her own business.
6. If absolutely necessary, they would consider using part of their $13,500 "emergency fund"

PUTTING IT ALL TOGETHER					
Financial Objectives					
College (1st Child)	College (2nd Child)	Home	Lifestyle (Auto)	Retirement	TOTALS FOR EACH YEAR
$ 612	$ 309	$ 2,809	$ 484	$ 3,696	$ 8,935
612	309	2,809	484	3,696	8,935
612	309	2,809	484	3,696	8,935
612	309	2,809		3,696	8,451
612	309	2,809		3,696	8,451
612	309	2,809		3,696	7,426
612	309	2,809		3,696	7,426
612	309	2,809		3,696	7,426
612	309			3,696	4,617
612	309			3,696	4,617
612	309			3,696	4,617
612	309			3,696	4,617
612	309			3,696	4,617
612	309			3,696	4,617
	309			3,696	4,005
	309			3,696	4,005
	309			3,696	4,005
	309			3,696	4,005
	309			3,696	4,005
	309			3,696	4,005
				3,696	3,696
				3,696	3,696
				3,696	3,696
				3,696	3,696
				3,696	3,696
				3,696	3,696
				3,696	3,696
				3,696	3,696
				3,696	3,696
				3,696	3,696
Total					
$8,568	$6,180	$22,472	$1,452	$110,880	$154,677

on a temporary basis to advance their savings/investment goals. They would do this knowing that they had backup funds of $26,000, devoted mainly to long-term goals, which they could dip into if an emergency occurred.

A Final Word

Two important points should be emphasized:

1. The Smith family's financial planning program has been designed for it, not for everyone. The Smiths' program demonstrates the way that financial planning works when it is applied to specific financial circumstances in order to achieve specific financial objectives. Since your circumstances and objectives will vary, so too will your means of achieving them—the financial planning program that you evolve for yourself.
2. As was the case with the Smiths, all those who shape their own financial planning program will find that they must adjust their goals to the reality of their circumstances. Starting a financial planning program early in life, when expenses are rising but peak levels of earning power have not yet been reached, inevitably and naturally involves a process of adjustment in which some goals must be changed and/or deferred. This adjustment process should take place with the recognition that deferred goals may be funded later as earning power increases.

INDEX

Note: Definitions of important terms appear on pages designated in boldface type.

Statistical Analysis

We chose three trial months for the measurement of the defined time stamps in the new process and consequently analyzed this data with different statistical tools in order to identify the highest leverage of action.

While streamlining the process and discussing different new options and opportunities for improvement, several hypothesis were established.

These hypotheses were tested with statistical hypothesis tests, whether the impression we had gained from the analysis was just an exceptional case or whether it was really some reason for the unstable or inefficient process. Soon it became clear that the processes in question involved far too many process loops and media interruptions. The person who ordered a software for example had to write an email. This information was fed in a workflow tool used by the IT Helpdesk, who in returned sent a paper copy of a form by the internal house mail to the person. This form had to be filled out and then to be signed by the superior. In other cases also the data owner or application responsible had to sign separate forms and then send them back via the internal mail. The result was then manually entered in the above mentioned workflow tool and in several other lists such as Excel lists etc. As easily could be seen, this process had streamlining potential.

When the impact of these loops was measured and could be made visible, it was not so hard to convince people to abolish certain process steps.

The New Way to Define the Process

In different creativity workshops and meetings we started to develop a new ordering system by putting the entire order process on the intranet (online forms) and to cut out all the time consuming loops. We still included for example the superior in the ordering loop – without, however, asking him or her for the signature anymore. The superior now receives a notification of the orders which his or her direct reports have been carried out. This was deemed to be sufficient as a valid monitoring instrument.

As soon as all measures have been defined the new, streamlined process has been mapped.

Communication and Implementation

Within the previously carried out stakeholder analysis, the people which had to be informed about the project as well as those people who would be affected by the new way of handling things, had to be informed. For that reason three presentations were organized (each attended by app. 20 people) and the new process was explained and questions were answered. This open and transparent communication has been highly appreciated.

After four months of defining, measuring, analyzing and improving, the implementation started. The new process started to be applied according to the new definitions and the measurements continued in order to check, whether the newly organized process had really improved the cycle time.

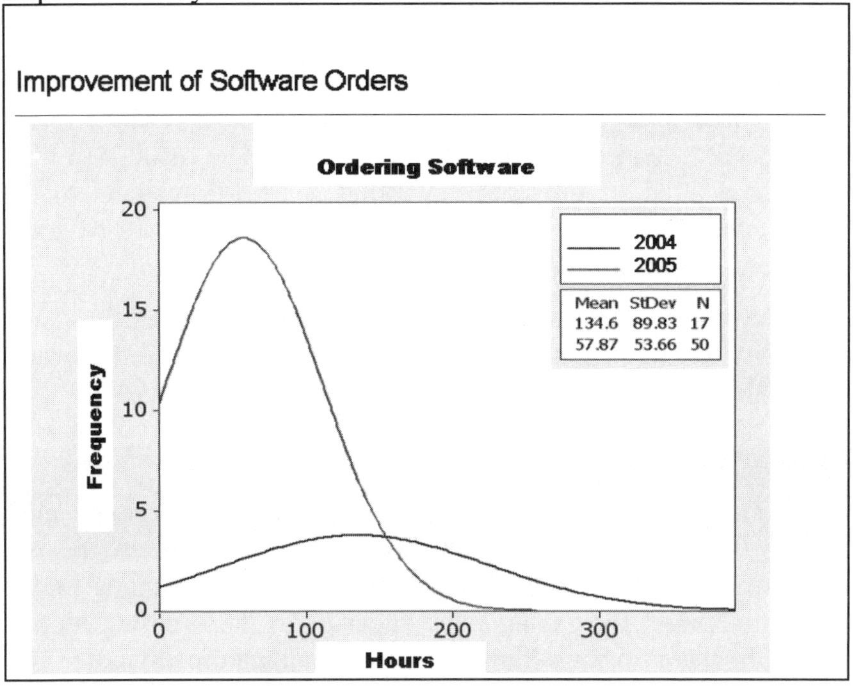

Fig. 8: Improvement of Orders 2004 - 2005

After three months of measuring the new process the first visible improvements could be shown. The delivery time of hardware orders had decreased by 18%, the of software orders even by 58% by improving the process itself. The variation of the process also decreased by 40%.

For the process of obtaining the rights for applications and access to data the average time period decreased by 55% and the variation improved by more than 70%.

Regarding the specification limits also an improvement could be made: In summer 2004 only 81% of the cases have been within the specification limits whereas in spring 2005 97% of all solutions have been found within the two required days. This was an improvement of 20% regarding the fulfillment of the specification limits.

These figures proved that the pilot project applying Six Sigma was successful. At this time more Six Sigma projects are being carried out.

What will be interesting is to continue to monitor the data also in the next months in order to check the sustainability of the processes and its improvements. In spring 2006 the next TRI*M survey is planned. These results will show whether the customers feel that the services of the IT Helpdesk have improved since the last time.

Learnings:

- A customer satisfaction survey is the base for any customer focused process analysis.
- Six Sigma always starts with a VoC, a very suitable tool being TRI*M.
- Continuous monitoring of the VoC, that is the TRI*M results is a prerequisite for sustainable success.

This shows very clearly that TRI*M and Six Sigma can be combined very well in order to meet the customers' needs better, to increase customer satisfaction and to streamline the process and make it more efficient.

Literature

Erwin, Jane; C Douglas; "Six Sigma's focus on total customer satisfaction"; Journal for Quality and Participation, Mar/Apr 2000

Harry Mike, Schroeder Richard; Six Sigma, „Prozesse optimieren, Null-Fehler Qualität schaffen, Rendite radikal steigern"; Campus NY; 2000

Janove W. Jonathan; "Society; Management by remote control: When managing employees in far-off locations, keep three ingredients: knowledge, trust and connectedness"; HR Magazine, April, 2004; Human Resource Management; Virginia; USA

Michael George L; "Lean Six Sigma for Service"; Mac Graw Hill Companies, 2003

Valeocon, Green Belt Theory Material, 2004

Wes Schotten; Hayes Group International; HR Magazine; Society for Human Resource Management; Virginia; USA; April 2004

www.isisxsigma.com; different articles and Six Sigma Dictionary

4 Public Sector TRI*M – Helping to Deliver Best Value

Mandy Littlewood, Anna Dudleston

4.1 Introduction

Local authorities throughout the UK have an obligation to strive towards continuous service improvements. In Scotland, these obligations are laid out in the Local Government in Scotland Act (2003). Local authorities are expected to monitor and measure their performance and deliver Best Value across the wide range of public services they offer.

Under the Act, local authorities have a duty to make arrangements that secure best value – that is, continuous improvement in the performance of the local authority's functions. In securing best value, the local authority is required to maintain an appropriate balance of quality in the performance of its functions and the cost of delivering that performance. Local authorities must deliver services with specific emphasis on efficiency; effectiveness; economy and the need to meet the equal opportunity requirements.

Nationally, the Audit Commission has also emphasised the need for residents surveys to determine not simply how satisfied customers are with services but to determine the extent to which customers' needs and expectations are being met.[1] The Audit Commission suggest a 'Gap Analysis' approach which measures actual performance against what a customer believes an 'excellent' service would offer. Though useful in some respects, the Audit Commission work starts from the position that each local authority must aim to deliver

---

[1] Audit Commission (1999) *Can't get no satisfaction*, Edinburgh

excellence in all that it does. Given the need to deliver Best Value in an efficient, effective and economic way, we would suggest the need to consider the extent to which customers consider services to be important. There is little point in delivering an excellent service in an area that customers do not think is a priority, if the impact might be a failure to deliver a satisfactory service in a more important area.

We wanted to deliver a methodology that helped local authorities to deliver Best Value but also recognised the budget constraints that authorities face in the choices they make. Striving for excellence in everything, while commendable, is not practical. We presented the TRI*M Model as a way of identifying public sector priorities.

The City of Edinburgh Council decided to use TRI*M to explore public perceptions and identify customers' service priorities, as part of an expanding programme of communication and consultation work. The Council recognised the importance of public perceptions in shaping and directing ongoing service developments and improvements. Therefore, the public perceptions work was a crucial component of not just performance monitoring but corporate planning in the medium and longer term.

While the annual tenant or residents survey has provided a great deal of important information, authorities have also become increasingly conscious of the limitations of the approach. This is particularly the case as the focus has shifted from simply measuring perceptions to trying to develop action plans and integrating customers' views into service and budget planning.

One of the main criticisms of the traditional satisfaction survey is that it focuses on service provision from the provider's perspective – how well are we doing what we do? – rather than from the perspective of the consumer. The model we proposed provides an opportunity to change this and identify the aspects of service provision that matter most to customers.

4.2 Study Objectives

The findings of the study were intended to directly inform the Council's proposed Annual Action Plans – setting out the detailed projects and programmes that will deliver the Corporate Plan. It was necessary to ensure that the public perceptions study clearly responded to and build on the key themes identified in the Corporate Plan.

The main objectives of the study were to:

- measure progress towards the achievement of the Council's strategic objectives
- monitor changes in perceptions and performance across time
- identify weaknesses in particular areas of existing service provision and so highlight priorities for improvement within services
- compare the performance of different services.

At the heart of the public sector the TRI*M Model is an assessment of residents' Overall Satisfaction with the Council's services and a measure of the importance and quality of the key aspects of the service. The analysis shows both the importance of individual service attributes and clients' perceptions of how well the Council is performing on these. In summary, the approach we adopted has the following characteristics.

- Measures performance on key indicators
- Identifies key attributes and measure performance
- Identifies customers' priorities and expectations
- Highlights areas for priority action
- Provides an understanding of the variation between different groups of residents
- Provides useful performance indicators to enable ongoing monitoring
- Links to customer care, staff training and communications strategies.

With these issues in mind, TNS Social designed and undertook a large-scale household survey with the purpose of examining public perceptions of the Council but with the added benefit of being able to identify the issues driving these perceptions and changes required to improve perceptions. Overall, 2,101 face-to-face interviews were undertaken by interviewers from TNS. Quotas were used to ensure that the sample of respondents closely reflected the profile of Edinburgh residents overall in terms of age, sex and working status. Around 350 interviews were undertaken in each of six administrative areas.

4.3 Developing the Service Priority Model

User surveys have traditionally focussed on attempting to measure what customers think of current service provision. This is usually done by asking them how satisfied they are with various aspects of the service provided to them by the Council. Although this is an important starting point, restricting this kind of research solely to examining satisfaction tends to produce findings that are difficult to interpret.

If, for example, 65% of respondents express satisfaction with the speed with which repairs are completed while only 35% say they are satisfied with the information provided about how repairs will be dealt with, the latter's lower satisfaction rating would seem to suggest that it requires more urgent attention. However, in the absence of information about the relative importance of each, there is no firm basis for that conclusion. It could be the case that the vast majority of respondents think that speed with which repairs are completed is crucial but do not consider information about how the repair will be dealt with to be at all important. Adding this dimension of importance allows us to provide meaningful interpretations of satisfaction scores and, thereby, identify priorities for action which will have the most significant impact on perceptions of service provision.

4.4 Identifying the Key Aspects of Service Provision

In order to identify which aspects of service provision have the greatest impact on respondents' opinions, TRI*M enables us to determine not only how satisfied residents are with various aspects of service provision but, crucially, how important these aspects are to them. By examining this second dimension of importance, gaps between expectations and day-to-day service provision could be identified and areas for action prioritised.

To allow us to use the TRI*M Analysis in the Council's survey, we asked questions about various aspects of service provision and, in relation to each, asked respondents to indicate how important each one is to them personally and how well they thought the Council performed in relation to each.

However, simply relying on how important respondents consider various aspects of service provision to be could be misleading. The factors that people say are important are not always the things that most influence their opinions. For example, if we were to talk to people about the important factors in their decision about purchasing a car, they might tell us that their new car must be environmentally-friendly. However, when it actually came time to buy the new car, it is likely that how environmentally-friendly it is would not, in fact, be an important consideration in the purchase decision.

To allow us to distinguish between what respondents say is important and what are the key factors that drive their attitudes and opinions, it is important to distinguish between two types of importance

1. Stated Importance – this is the importance that respondents place on the various attributes of service provision when asked directly about them i.e. what respondents say is important to them in the questionnaire.

2. Impact on Real Relevance – this is the impact each of these attributes has on respondents' opinions of the Council. This dimension of importance is derived from statistical analysis and cannot be asked explicitly of respondents.

4.5 Interpreting the Results of the Model

The key to our approach is producing output that is easy for Council staff to interpret and highlights key areas for action, factors often lacking in traditional attitude research. To explain the survey results in relation to the two dimensions of importance outlined above, we created classic TRI*M Grids in two-dimensional space as shown in figure 1.

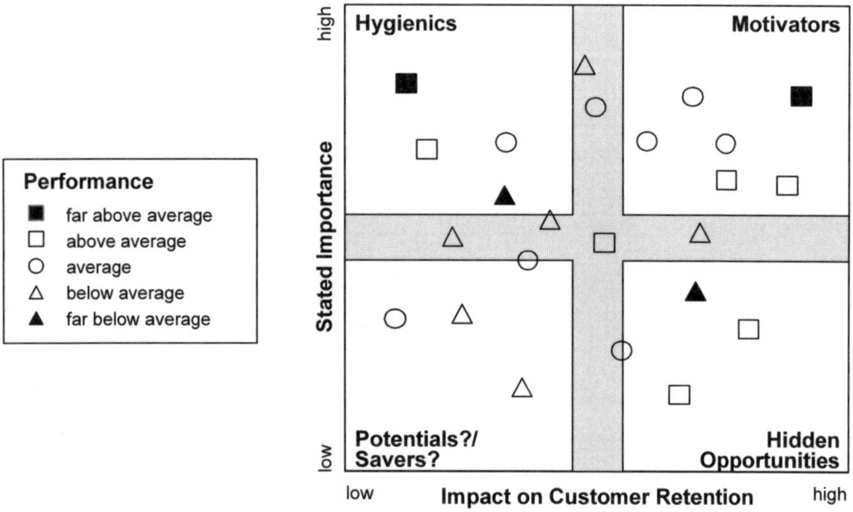

*Fig. 1: The Analysis TRI*M Grid*

As shown in figure 1, this two-dimensional space (or Analysis TRI*M Grid) is segmented into four quadrants, each having specific relevance to respondents' attitudes towards and opinions of the Council –

- Motivators – in this quadrant, both Stated Importance and Real Relevance are high. Attributes which fall into this quadrant are not only rated as being important by respondents when asked about them directly in the questionnaire but are also shown by statistical analysis to have a real impact on their attitudes. Attributes falling into this quadrant are crucial to respondents' perceptions of the service provided to them by the Council. An example might be the effectiveness of street cleaning.

- Hidden Opportunities – although not generally perceived as important (i.e. having a low Stated Importance), these attributes are, in fact, shown to have a real impact on respondents. These represent real opportunities to impact positively on attitudes towards the Council. An example might be the ways the Council communicates with its residents.
- Hygienics – these are the areas that respondents often rate as highly important (i.e. Stated Importance is high), however, analysis shows they actually have relatively little impact on attitudes and opinions (i.e. Real Relevance is low). These attributes basically represent the essentials of service delivery. An example might be providing street lighting, once the basics have been provided, further improvement has limited impact.
- Potentials?/Savers? – in this quadrant, both Stated Importance and Real Relevance are low. Attributes falling into this quadrant have little impact on respondents' perceptions of service delivery. An example might be having good facilities in Council offices.

The next stage is to map the various attributes onto this Analysis TRI*M Grid according to their Stated Importance (which determines their position on the y-axis) and Real Relevance (which determines their position on the x-axis).

The final stage is to assign a symbol to each attribute that shows how respondents rated the Council's performance on the particular attribute.

4.6 Analysing the Council's Performance

In the analysis of results we first consider the overall service provided by the Council as a whole – looking at the relative importance and perceived performance of a whole range of Council services to assess overall service priorities. We then examine specific services or sets of services to assess service priorities and improvements for the different Council services. As the TRI*M Model works by assessing the relative importance of attributes against each other, in some cases the services will be positioned and rated differently within the Overall TRI*M Grid and the service specific Grids.

Figure 1 summarises the relative performance of a range of Council services and how the different attributes of these services impact on Overall Satisfaction with the Council. The aim is to look behind the views on satisfaction and value for money to see which factors drive these views. The TRI*M Grid shown is based on the forty different service elements shown in the key below the Grid. The elements span several different Council departments and services but do not include all services provided by the Council.

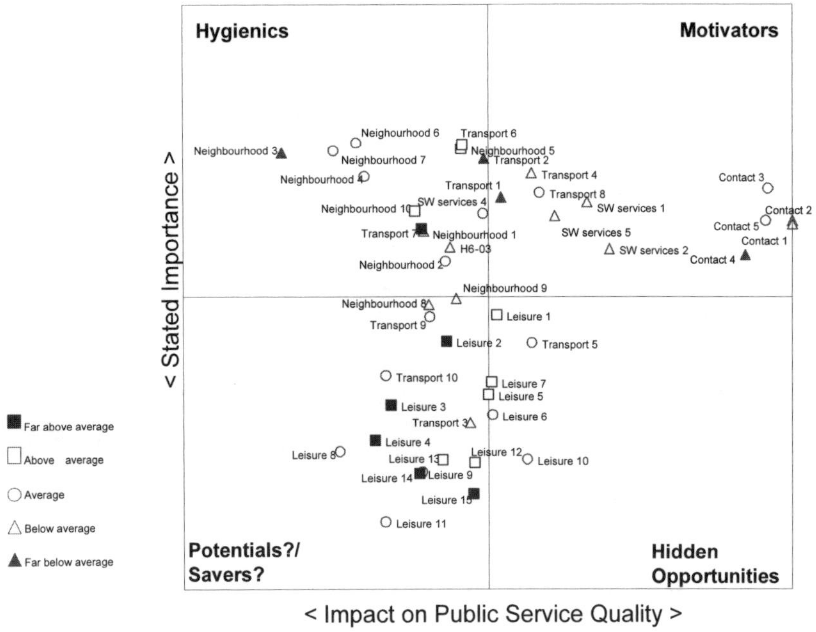

*Fig. 2: TRI*M Grid for All Residents*

Key to Services

Neighbourhood issues	Travel and transport issues
Neighbour 1 Area free of litter **Neighbour 2** Grassy areas tidy and well kept **Neighbour 3** Area free of dog dirt **Neighbour 4** Free of vandalism/graffiti **Neighbour 5** Vermin/pests controlles **Neighbour 6** Feel safe walking at night **Neighbour 7** Low risk of burglary/car crime **Neighbour 8** Somewhere for children to play **Neighbour 9** Jobs for local people **Neighbour 10** Local shops and services	**Transport 1** Maintenance of roads **Transport 2** Maintenance of footpaths and pavements **Transport 3** Providing and maintaining cycle ways **Transport 4** Snow/ice-clearing and gritting **Transport 5** Financial support for buses **Transport 6** Maintaining street lighting **Transport 7** School crossing patrols **Transport 8** Improving road safety **Transport 9** 20mph and traffic calming **Transport 10** Regulating and enforcing parking restrictions
Contacting the Council	**Care services**
Contact 1 You can get things done with a quick phone call **Contact 2** It is clear who to contact for queries **Contact 3** Staff know how to deal with queries	**SW services 1** Support at home for vulnerable/elderly **SW services 2** Access to housing and housing support **SW services 3** Work between agencies to support children

Contact 4 The Council keeps you informed about ongoing problems or queries **Contact 5** Things are explained in plain language	**SW services 4** Support for children with disabilities **SW services 5** Support for children who cannot live with their own families
Leisure and learning	

Leisure 1	Parks
Leisure 2	Library
Leisure 3	Museums
Leisure 4	Theatres
Leisure 5	Sports Centres
Leisure 6	Playgrounds
Leisure 7	Swimming pools
Leisure 8	Sports pitches
Leisure 9	Community Centres
Leisure 10	Out of school activities
Leisure 11	Public Internet Access
Leisure 12	Adult Education
Leisure 13	Learning opportunities
Leisure 14	Festivals
Leisure 15	Christmas events

In terms of service provision, six service elements are rated far above average (in relation to the other services provided by the Council) as represented by a black square in the Grid. They are as follows:

- Organising Christmas Events – The 'Capital Christmas' and Hogmanay
- Organising Festivals throughout the year
- Theatres
- Libraries
- Museums
- School crossing patrols

Conversely, the Council are rated as well below average (in relation to their provision of other services) in relation to four elements – indicated on the Grid by a dark triangle. These service elements are as follows:

- The Council keeping individual residents informed about ongoing problems or queries
- Maintenance of roads
- Maintenance of footpaths and pavements
- Keeping areas free from dog dirt

Service Priorities

However, knowing which service elements the Council is seen as performing above and below average is not enough to decide which services should be prioritised in order to increase satisfaction. The Council might be seen as excellent at organising the Edinburgh Festival and Hogmanay events but this particular element is not a key driver of Overall Satisfaction.

The key to using the Grid to target service improvements is to focus on elements most likely to impact on Overall Satisfaction (those in the top right quadrant or near the border) which the are currently perceived to be performing poorly (blank or black triangle). For longer term planning, it would also be prudent for the Council to look at plans for improving those which are currently average (a circle) and make sure those which are currently performing well are maintained at their current levels.

Additionally, it is well worth considering giving priority to elements which fall into the 'Hidden Opportunities' quadrant (bottom right quadrant) although not generally perceived as important (i.e. having a low Stated Importance), these attributes are, in fact, shown to have a real impact on respondents. These represent real opportunities to impact positively on attitudes towards the Council.

From figure 3 this means that the following service elements should be prioritised for improvement as they are currently seen as performing poorly (well below average) and are clear drivers of Overall Satisfaction:

- The Council keeps you informed about ongoing queries or problems
- Maintenance of roads
- Maintenance of pavements and footpaths

Next level priority should be given to elements currently performing below average and in or near the top right quadrant:

- Being able to get things done quickly with a telephone call
- It being clear who to contact about specific problems or queries
- Having access to the right kind of housing and housing support to meet needs
- Support at home and in the community for vulnerable and older people
- Support for children who can't live with their own families

Clearly, the response to these issues has differential budget impacts, with the need to provide more information to residents with ongoing queries or problems having less resource implication than spending on the maintenance of roads and footpaths across the city, for instance.

Several elements relating to the provision of services to vulnerable people within the community appear in the list above. However, it is probable that many residents perceptions of these services are not based on experience - it might be that priority needs to be given to raising awareness of the support provided is needed rather than necessarily considerable changes made to service provision. A high proportion of respondents said they did not know how well the Council performed in relation to such services.

There are also some attributes that appear to be key overall drivers of satisfaction for which the Council currently performs averagely. Improvement in these areas could have a positive impact on Overall Satisfaction.

- Improving road safety
- Having Council staff who know how to deal with queries
- Having things explained in plain language

There are also three service elements in the 'Hidden Opportunities' quadrant which appear to have a correlation with Overall Satisfaction but for which the Council is currently performing at an average level as follows:

- Financial support for buses
- Playgrounds
- Out of school activities (sports, play schemes, homework clubs)

Although service elements fall into either the 'Hygienics' or 'Potentials?/Savers?'quadrants does NOT mean that they are not important services – it rather means that they have relatively little impact on attitudes and opinions – for example, improving museums is not likely to have a positive impact on Overall Satisfaction with the Council.

Specific Services

Here we have separately presented the detailed analysis conducted for the Council in three key service areas – neighbourhood services, contacting the Council and travel and transport.

Neighbourhood Services

The TRI*M Grid below shows the relative importance of the various neighbourhood attributes and services included in the questionnaire, as well as how highly they were rated by residents (indicated by the various symbols – see key next to Grid).

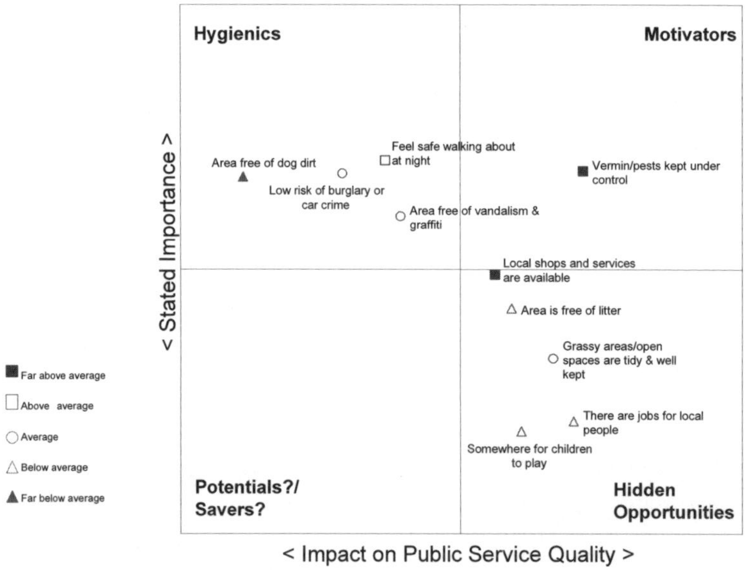

*Fig. 3: TRI*M Grid for Neighbourhood Characteristics and Services*

As shown in figure 3, aspects of the neighbourhood emerge as very important overall, with no attributes in the 'Potentials?/Savers?' quadrant. In fact, neighbourhood or community related issues tend to cluster in the 'Hygienics' and Hidden Opportunity' quadrants. These are key areas to maintain or increase investment, particularly in relation to the 'Hidden Opportunities'; the area being free of litter, jobs for local people and there being somewhere for children to play.

These were all rated relatively poorly (as indicated by the triangle symbols). Further, although these three areas were not rated as being as important as other aspects of their local neighbourhood by residents (they have relatively low Stated Importance), in fact, statistical analysis shows that these areas do appear to have an impact on Overall Satisfaction with the Council. Thus improving these areas should have a positive impact on overall perceptions of Council services.

Contact with the Council

A key area of customer care is the contact and communication between the Council and residents. Figure 4 shows the relative performance of the Council in terms of contact with residents. Communication with the Council was rated relatively poorly in terms of enabling residents to get things done with a quick 'phone call, and satisfaction with this factor impacted on residents' Overall Satisfaction. This suggests that focusing on to the time taken to deal with (simple) queries would have a beneficial impact on resident's perception of the Council. There would also be some benefits in providing more or clearer information about which department to contact for different types of problem as better performance on this would be likely to improve Overall Satisfaction levels.

Although being kept informed about ongoing issues does not have a significant impact on Overall Satisfaction, it is an area that the Council is performing less well in and therefore may wish to review. This measure may also relate the 'getting things done with a quick 'phone call issue. If the Council resolves the responsiveness during phone calls, the need for better performance in relation to ongoing issues becomes less important.

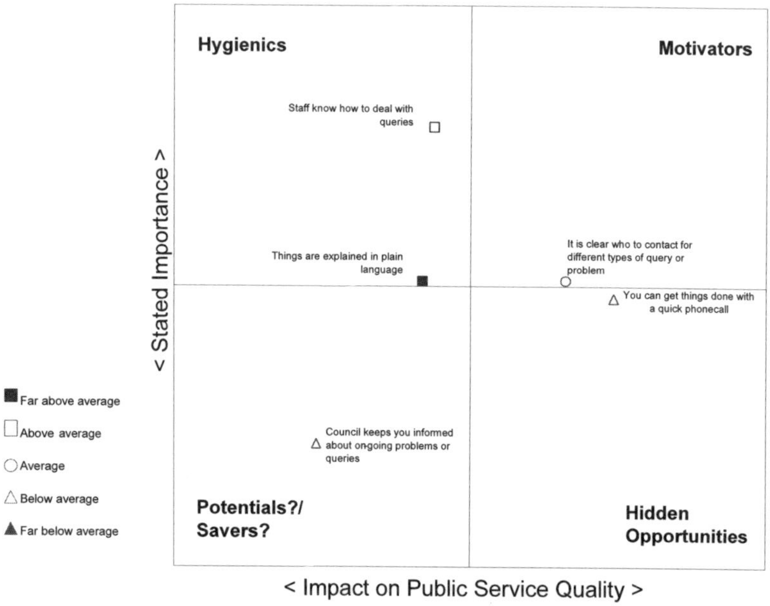

*Fig. 4: TRI*M Grid Relating to Contact with the Council*

Travel and Transport

The Grid for travel and transport issues shows good performance on two 'Hygienics' services - the provision of school crossing patrols and maintaining street lighting. Most other services are considered to be 'average' except maintenance of roads and maintenance of footpaths that are well below average. These are key areas for future investment. More investment in snow and ice clearing/gritting and improving road safety may also improve these areas to above average scores. Also, in terms of the relative importance of policies, the Council may take the view that improving road safety directly and by virtue of winter snow and ice clearing and gritting is more important. Improving these services alongside the ongoing maintenance of pavements, footpaths and roads is likely to have a clear impact on Overall Satisfaction.

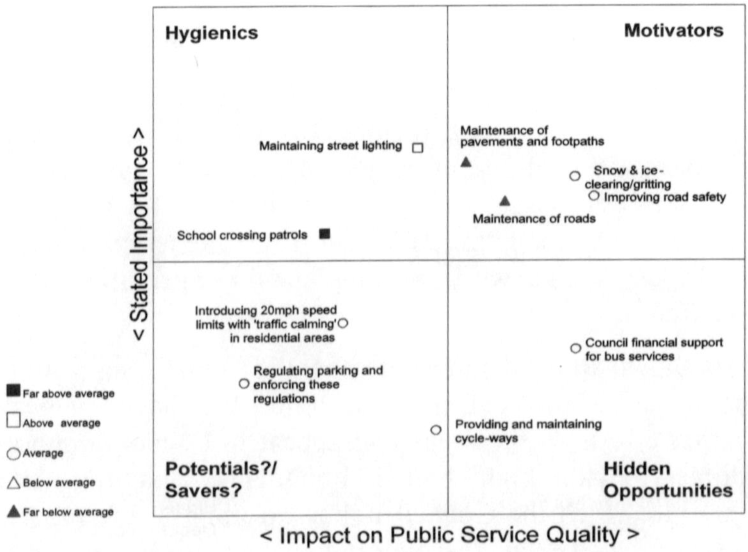

*Fig. 5: TRI*M Grid for Travel and Transport Services*

Council financial support for bus services appears to have lower Stated Importance but high Real Relevance. The Council is only rated as 'average' in provision of this service so it is important to make sure service in this area is at least maintained (if not improved) as it does have an impact on Overall Satisfaction.

The positioning of the introduction of 20 mph speed limits and regulating and enforcing parking relations in the bottom left quadrant of the Grid indicates that the Council's performance in these areas may not have a significant impact on resident's overall attitudes and opinions. This does not mean that it is not an important issue – particularly for some residents – just that it is not likely to impact greatly on overall perceptions of the Council's Overall Performance.

Conclusions

In the provision of local services, local authorities are in the unenviable position of being required to allocate scarce public resources in an efficient and effective way across a wide range of competing services. Local authorities also need to fulfil their commitment to continuous improvement in public services and the delivery of Best Value, while keeping public expenditure within reasonable limits.

The results shown above demonstrate how the Council can prioritise resources in the short and medium term. We have suggested concentrating efforts of the areas that appear to be most important for customers (with high Stated Importance and high Real Relevance) but which the Council is not excelling at the moment. We have also suggested secondary emphasis to be placed on 'Hidden Opportunities'.

Of course, local authorities always need to counterbalance their own strategic and policy objectives alongside public opinion. It may be that political imperatives mean that resources need to be directed towards some 'Hygienics' or 'Potentials?/Savers?' areas. These may be key policy areas, such as traffic calming in residential areas, improving communication with customers and tackling crime and fear of crime.

This paper shows how the TRI*M Analysis can also be used to inform the budgeting priorities local authorities must make, allowing them to spend their available resources in areas that would appear to be of most concern to local residents and impact most on their views of the Council's performance. Using TRI*M as a service prioritisation tool can, therefore, directly contribute to the goals of continuous improvement and the delivery of Best Value services.

5 Customer Satisfaction with Commerzbank's Retail Banking

Michael Schroth

5.1 10 Years of TRI*M – A Report of Past Experiences

5.1.1 TRI*M Development Process Within the Commerzbank

For more than ten years now, Commerzbank has used the TRI*M Monitoring Tool in a very successful way.

However, a tool like TRI*M is similar to a small autonomous company, that is, in order to be successful it cannot afford to ignore constant change, but rather, has to be continually adapted to changing conditions on both the customers' and the corporation's side. Even though basic aims remain largely unchanged, episodic structural changes and the processes of adaptation that result in the "large" corporation, influence this small TRI*M company on a multitude of levels.

It is for this reason, that I would like to discuss in this document, the process of development of this tool in our corporation; including necessary adjustments, related problems, and their solutions. It is my intention to describe to the reader, very simple practical steps, for day-to-day working with this tool; moreover, I am confident that at several points in this document, some TRI*M users will recognise their own queries, problems and experiences.

TRI*M's methodical approach is undoubtedly excellent; but, this type of tool can only continue to thrive and survive in a corporation, if the necessary and frequently quite simple steps required for targeted application and implementation, are continuously used and adjusted in a pragmatic manner; and more importantly, geared towards sales.

We started out with a company-wide TRI*M study in 1993. In the first year, we had representative, very interesting results indeed, based on a survey across the whole banking group. Due to the relatively large sample, of approximately 3,000 surveyed customers, we were able to analyse the data using all the classic approaches, thus enabling a split into different sub-groups of targeted criteria, e.g. sociodemographic and bank-specific segment criteria such as customer types, revenue categories and product usage.

In the case of banking-specific analysis criteria it was of course necessary to include these attributes to the survey - either beforehand or afterwards - using internal databases, as customers were not always aware of these details or not able to disclose these details, or indeed not willing to divulge them.

This procedure happened on two levels, whereby the sampling process was initially split in line with our targeted sales-groups, namely: individual customers, retail customers and small business customers. The need to achieve an adequate response rate for "smaller" segments, which would include in our case small business customers, was an important reason for this approach.

Information relating to customers' product usage or annual revenue was only merged into the raw data after the end of fieldwork, for the benefit of Data Protection (DP). Although it would obviously be better to simply include the data as fields of the individual record during the sampling process, this was at that time not possible, either for reasons related to DP (e.g. the sampling application accessed different urns of source data), or, in any case the procedure had had to be done over the course of two sampling runs.

Furthermore, it made also more sense to merge in data - related to the customer's annual revenue for the running year - at the end of the year, i.e. at the point when the TRI*M Survey data was actually analysed, rather than during sampling, as annual revenue can only be determined at the end of the year; or as may be the case, is much simpler to estimate based on 10 months rather than just 3 to 4 months.

Up to the present day, we have kept the structure of content for this company-wide banking survey largely unchanged. Although adjustments relating to specific details within the list of questions (e.g. modifications/ additions to performance/ rating criteria) were obviously made during the course of previous years.

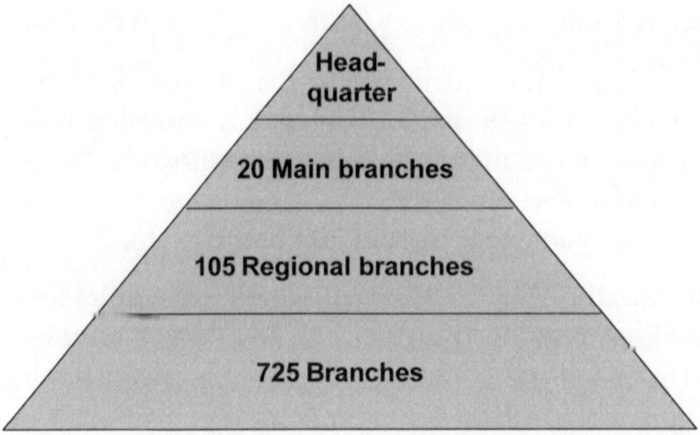

*Fig. 1: Form and Structure of Commerzbank's TRI*M Survey*

Commerzbank's retail banking sector has for quite some time been controlled via regional sales units: regional headquarters, main regional branch and local branch (see: figure 1, for Commerzbank's Regional Sales Structure).

Most marketing or sales managers are painfully aware of how the findings and assessments of company-wide surveys are received by the individual sales units when it comes to monitoring these units. Naturally, this applies not only to findings derived from customer satisfaction surveys, even though some target segments can be separated out; on each occasion the following problems continually arise.

Naturally, sales managers responsible for a specific sales unit (e.g. regional branch areas) always view their own units as performing much better than "that" company-wide average, which has always been brought down by "some other" (worse-performing) sales units. Unfortunately, with the findings from a survey that collects data across the whole of a corporation, this sentiment cannot be disproved.

Even when results are broken down into areas (Commerzbank has a total of 20 areas reporting to their main regional branches), the range can vary to such a great extent based both on regions and the branches within them. Thus, it is clearly not possible to assume low ratings for all regions or branches within an area, based on a low rating for the overall area.

This meant that, in order to use TRI*M as a monitoring tool also in the sales context, it was imperative that regional results needed to be split by sales units far more strictly – by branch areas if at all possible, and at the very least by regional branch areas.

This was then, a very important step, which we implemented two years after the general commencement of TRI*M at Commerzbank.

We have retained the option of splitting by region until the present day – albeit with a number of stronger modifications.

Apart from the two "classic" Commerzbank customer satisfaction surveys (company-wide TRI*M and regional TRI*M), we also established in the years that followed a TRI*M Survey for our subsidiary: comdirect-Bank.

Six years ago the "retail banking" business sector, set up a customer satisfaction survey that is now repeated at regular intervals. We have also conducted product-specific TRI*M Surveys (see figure 2) for

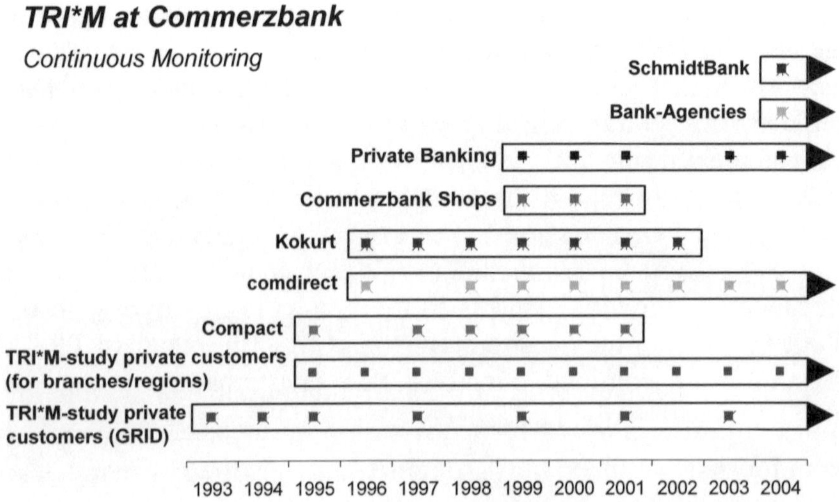

Fig. 2

certain complex products e.g. standardised asset management (Compact). It is not my intention to discuss these specific "customizations" of our TRI*M Surveys within the Commerzbank group any further. I have merely mentioned them for the sake of being comprehensive; in order to illustrate that at Commerzbank we are using the TRI*M Methodology in both a very intensive and far-reaching manner.

The main intention of my article is to provide a detailed sketch of the development and questions and problems that arose due to the practical implementation of TRI*M in the business sector of retail banking. Finally, I will give a brief outline of those future applications that are currently planned.

Our company-wide TRI*M Survey was initially based on postal questionnaires, which presented itself as a "cost-saving" alternative for the years to come, particularly compared to the very extensive survey at branch-level, due to the raw sample).

For the survey at branch-level, the raw sample had to be increased by several multiples, in order to achieve a result of at least 100 responses per branch (which was our minimum requirement for analysis).

As a result, we posted a total of more than 800,000 letters to our customers in 1995, the year we began analysis of the TRI*M Survey down to branch-level. At the same time, the questionnaire differentiated between the company-wide survey and the branch survey. In the context of the TRI*M Grid, we asked questions regarding the importance of aspects in the company-wide question-naires only – the so-called “long version”. There were generally between 2000 and 3000 completed questionnaires. We no longer asked about the relevance of individual aspects in the branch-level surveys. In this “short version” of the questionnaire, apart from the standard TRI*M Questions, we confined ourselves two questions concerning the satisfaction with individual aspects.

This obviously assumed (an assumption duly justified by many years of experience) that the relevance of aspects was almost identical amongst Commerzbank customers throughout Germany. We were also able to support this assumption with the fact that, with respect to aspects, no notable differences were apparent between different federal states in regional splits; based on the sample of the company-wide survey.

As is usually the case with postal surveys, response rates proved to be a fundamental problem. To ensure a representative spread as well as for reasons of cost, we were naturally concerned to achieve as high a response rate as possible. Meaning, that we had to increase the respondents’ motivation to complete and post the questionnaire by, for example, offering incentives. With this in mind, we tested several alternatives during the first years of TRI*M Surveys at branch-level.

The initial incentive concept we employed for the postal survey proved very costly (both in financial terms and in terms of time consumed) and was a prize-draw for very valuable prizes indeed. This concept, however, resulted in the highest response rates achieved.

In one year, for example, the first prize in the draw was a Mercedes and the second and third prizes were holidays abroad. In this specific case we were able to achieve an average response rate well in excess of 20%.

During the following years, we "only" offered holidays as the top three prizes and some smaller prizes consisted of consumer goods. Here, the response rate was still over 15%. In both of these scenarios, however, the expense of processing was very high (apart from the direct cost of the incentives, considerable resources in terms of personnel and time were needed to be committed). For this reason, these types of incentives were discontinued in the years that followed (largely due to reasons of limited capacities in terms of personnel, and the highly complex administrative requirements entailed; rather than due to considerations of cost).

In subsequent years, we mostly worked with altruistic incentives: donations to charitable organisations. Customers were informed in the covering letter, that we would donate a fixed amount (usually between 1-3 Euros) to a charitable institution for each returned questionnaire.

With this approach, the response rates were no longer quite as high, but still reached 10 to 12%. One reason for us to continue with these kinds of incentives to this day was the limited amount of time required to internally administrate them.

In addition to this, we were able to market these incentives in terms of PR (e.g. press releases regarding the handing over a cheque to a particular charitable institution); which is definitely an advantage in terms of our public image.

During the postal survey, we tested a concept for the so-called "short version" of the questionnaire, which involved a slightly enlarged postcard (nonetheless, in a stamped return envelope). Behind this was the hypothesis that the shorter and simpler the questionnaire, the higher the response rate. This however, did not in fact turn out to be the case. This reply card consisted of only 4 TRI*M Questions and the 6 most important aspects from the Commerzbank's TRI*M Grid as its content, really very short, and completion would take a respondent under three minutes.

In spite of this, the response rate reached only 8% and consequently was far lower than expected. The agency conducting the survey, TNS Infratest, believes that a possible reason for this is may be an assumption by many customers of a low importance with regard to the topic at hand, due to the very fact that it is presented to them in postcard format; and thus they decide not to bother to reply, as they do not deem completion to be of any importance.

This experience made us decide to revert in the years that followed to the original format, of two A4-sized pages; and this is the very format that we have continued to employ, in our postal surveys up to the present day.

During the course of 2000 and 2001, Commerzbank's branch network underwent a period of downsizing and structural change.

On the one hand, more than 200 branches were closed or merged with other branches; while on the other, specific consulting services (e.g. mortgages) were combined in so-called consultation centres, so that one consultation centre could be responsible for several branches.

As a matter of course, this had considerable consequences for our survey, which had to be adjusted both in terms of sampling and analysis. We could now no longer be certain, when we asked a customer about their satisfaction or dissatisfaction, whether a low rating at the TRI*M Questions was due to negative experiences at their account-holding branch (the branch at which the customers generally conduct their business), or whether this was due to a bad consultation received from a consultation centre.

While it would most definitely have been possible, to portray these structural changes in the questionnaire while incorporating an appropriate method of differentiation, this, however, would also have entailed difficulties in terms of survey methodology and would probably not have been wholly comprehensible from the customers' perspective. As well as making the questionnaire less clearly structured, it would have also increased the survey's length even further; such changes would constitute a considerable hindrance to the postal survey's response rate.

There is also though, another consideration: the expense of posting the letters containing the questionnaires. In 2000, we achieved a total of approximately 130,000 returned responses, from a mail-out of slightly less than a million letters.

In 2001, taking the aforementioned into account, we completely revised the survey in conjunction with TNS Infratest with respect to sampling (both in terms of sample size and structure).

Commerzbank used to have well in excess of 900 branches, but following restructuring this figure has dropped to 725. These branches are assigned to regions, and dependant on size each region comprises 5-10 branches, and 1-2 consultation centres, which contain highly trained specialists with responsibilities for more complex consultations (e.g. mortgages, fund/asset management) and for the customers of all branches of the region in question. These regions themselves were combined into a total of 20 areas (see illustration 1).

We then decided to make these regions, numbering a total of 105 (=areas of main regional branches), the smallest unit of analysis and no longer the branches themselves, as had previously been the case.

We wanted to achieve a minimum of 100 valid interviews in each of these regions. Thus, we were aiming for a total of at least 11,000 completed interviews per year.

This was a tenth of what we previously had to process and spent on postage.

Each of the head branches of our 20 areas (these are the sales areas, each of which is responsible for several regions) received the results for the separate regions in their area.

These results indicated, with regard to the TRI*M Index, the 4 separate TRI*M Questions and the most important performance-related aspects, on the one hand the changes of the individual regions compared to the previous year; and on the other hand deviations from the overall average, across the whole of the company (see figure 3).

This regional level of analysis has also been retained to the present day.

5.1.2 Postal Surveys or Telephone Surveys?

One topic, which was a subject of regular discussion at our company, was the form of conducting interviews. We started TRI*M as a postal survey. In the years to come, fieldwork by phone was also considered as an alternative, but time and again we decided against this approach. Partly due to the increased cost (which, in hindsight, would really not have been that excessive), but also due to the possibility of negative reactions from customers (passing on contact details to a market research agency is a sensitive topic, especially when it comes to the customers of banks).

However, in 2001, in spite of these concerns, we decided to try and conduct part of our customer satisfaction survey by phone.

In order to alleviate the problem of the sensitivity over the passing on of contact details, the customers selected during the sampling process, received written information in advance. This stated that they were to be contacted by TNS Infratest during the course of the following weeks, and asked to participate in an interview. The customers were offered the option to call a hotline, prominently displayed in the letter, in order to either refuse participation or to gain further information about the survey from Commerzbank.

Contrary to our initial expectations, with only a few exceptions, customer reaction was moderate. Relatively few customers requested to be removed from the survey, and others – the majority in fact – wanted simply to get more detailed information e.g. confirmation that the survey was genuinely anonymous.

Additionally, some customers directly called their consultant at their local branch (naturally, consultants had been internally informed regarding the survey) to confirm that it was a bona fide enterprise i.e. a legitimate survey sponsored by Commerzbank. Proactive consultants geared towards sales, used this opportunity to talk to the customers about new offers – which was quite a pleasant side effect from the point of view of sales.

The phone number cited in the letter, connected callers to our call centre, which had received in advance documentation relevant to the exercise, containing both potential queries that might arise, and corresponding answers to these. Over the years, we were able to fine-tune this documentation to such an extent, that the call centre is now pre-prepared for almost any queries a customer might have.

Only a very small number of calls were received from annoyed customers seeking to complain about our intention to pass on their contact details to a market research agency. Yet even with these individuals, it was possible to either change their perspective during the course of the telephone conversation; or at least offer them some reassurance.

TNS Infratest then conducted a total of 36,000 telephone interviews for Commerzbank during 2001, which constituted a response rate of almost 50% of the total sample. With this kind of response rate, sample distribution by specific regions or target segments was superior to that encountered with postal surveys; which proved to be a considerable advantage, as it resulted in significantly less effort being required for weighting the data.

As a result, we currently conduct our TRI*M Survey partly by phone and partly using postal questionnaires.

Nevertheless, the postal survey still constitutes a slightly lesser expense, as the telephone interviews also involve informing prospective respondents in writing, and thus incur both postage and telephony costs; as opposed to the sole cost of just a letter and return postage. (Notwithstanding the fact of a much larger mail-out volume due to an expected response rate of less than 10%). Nonetheless, the amount of internal time required for conducting a postal survey is much higher, which is a fact frequently neither precisely considered or factored, when calculating overall costs.

There is also, apart from cost, another important reason for continuing to conduct part of our TRI*M Survey by post.

As part of our internal data mining efforts at Commerzbank, we aim to continually feed information about our customers' satisfaction into our 'data mart' on a 1:1 basis (not via a data matching model – more on this later!); in order to, for example, directly identify dissatisfied customers and react appropriately.

This direct feed of satisfaction-related information also enables us to improve our lost-customer index; which is continually calculated as part of our data mining efforts.

In addition to this, we have provided the option for customers of a tick-box within the postal survey, to indicate if they want to be contacted by their consultant – irrespective of whether they are satisfied or not.

Customer IDs are printed on the postal questionnaires, and this visibility to the customer, increases their awareness that data is not collected in an anonymous manner. In addition, this is also implied by the above-mentioned option for the customers to tick whether they wanted to be contacted by their consultant.

For customers who tick this question, we provide in the DP-based sales-information system corresponding information to the relevant customer service representatives at branch-level. They can then contact these customers directly, and thus will also be provided with a good basis for a cross-selling conversation.

Additionally, we have also combined sales-information with a corresponding remark to the relevant consultants responsible, for all customers who have ticked "less than satisfied" or "dissatisfied" at the question asking about satisfaction. In this case also, through the ensuing conversation, the consultants have been tasked with approaching the customers and establishing the reasons for their rating. We have had quite positive reactions from this approach, as with the method mentioned above.

In many cases, it was possible to resolve the concerning issues during an open conversation, and quite often, this conversation has been successfully used to sell another financial product, or to increase the present level of assets.

In this regard, we have been able to make an observation based on further analysis; or rather we have been able to confirm a finding that will surely be familiar to experts in the area of TQM. Notably, dissatisfied customers, who had a conversation with their consultants, did not leave in the following quarter. Conversely, as expected, we found that the rate of lost customers during the quarter following the survey was decidedly above average, amongst those dissatisfied customers who were not approached by their consultants (in comparison with normally incurred customer loss).

However, amongst those that were approached, we recorded a notably higher rate of lost customers in the next quarter: which apparently occurred in cases where the conversation with the consultant did not lead to either a positive development or action.

For us, this is an indication, particularly in the context of our complaints management procedure, that it is crucial to take ownership for a problem resolution, both in a timely and satisfactory manner, from the customers' perspective.

Using this approach, in addition to its purpose as a tool for making both strategic and tactical business decisions, we have created the opportunity of utilising the TRI*M Survey in day-to-day operations, in a successful targeted manner.

Another application made possible by the postal (non-anonymous) survey, is the capability now to, for instance, observe how within our company dissatisfied customers are dealt with during the course of time. In this way, we can precisely monitor at what point in time, which of these customers terminate their business, cancel certain products, or withdraw larger assets.

As expected, an initial analysis showed that dissatisfied customers much more frequently terminated their business i.e. they completely cut all ties to the bank. In numerous cases (although at this stage this is still a hypothesis) it appears that they initiate this "process of disassociation" with the cancelling of individual products and a reduction in the size of their assets.

By utilising the information that a customer's dissatisfaction is most likely a reason for his or her action, we are able to influence this development through the consultant; and, in many cases, facilitate positive change.

5.1.3 Communicating the Results

Communicating the results in a manner geared towards different audiences, is of paramount importance for implementing the results and findings of the TRI*M Survey. At Commerzbank, this is facilitated by using both centralised and decentralised approaches.

Principally, the executive management at company headquarters, are presented with the overall results at the end of the year, which is combined with particularly interesting findings which relate to individual segments (e.g. customers split by product usage, revenue, or length of business relationship). The consequence of the presentation of these results, are assignments, designed for the different specialised sub-divisions of our retail banking business, whose aim is the central initiation and implementation of corresponding company-wide measures e.g. the modification or supplementation of training/coaching programmes, changes or additions to product features, and so on. One measure implemented within the area of current accounts, for example, was to switch the account statement's size to A4; after it was recognised that the comprehensibility of these statements (hygienic aspect), was rated poorly over the course of several consecutive years: due to the limitations in the amount of text that could be shown, on the smaller statement slips.

Splitting by levels of revenue can lead to interesting findings with regard to the sub-segments, as part of the analysis of company-wide results. Generally speaking, it is found that customers with higher levels of revenue also have higher commitment ratings; but they also show very quick and sensitive reactions to negative developments.

It is as a consequence of this, that we noted a very sharp drop in customer satisfaction amongst our highly profitable customers with stock portfolios, during the poor stock market results of both 2001 and 2002.

Naturally, as part of this centralised presentation, regional developments are also covered.

We find again and again in this context, that in the business of banking: customer retention and customer satisfaction are largely shaped by the local branches and their employees. Consequently in 2003, a range varying from 35 to 75 was exhibited by the TRI*M Index of our regional branch areas. Therefore, the sales managers at company headquarters, with responsibilities for certain areas, have clear points to start from, in approaching their regional executives in a focussed manner.

Of equal, if not greater importance, to the informing of the executive management is the communication of these findings to the regional sales teams; as this is where the majority of the findings derived from the results, are actually implemented. The main drivers of customer satisfaction take effect at a local level.

As I have mentioned already, Commerzbank no longer splits its results by branch, but by the 105 regions each comprised of between 5 to 10 branches.

Each of these regions (for which a main regional branch manager is responsible) receives once a year the results of the sales area covered, shown both in comparison with, the other regions within the whole branch area, and also in relation to, developments in the previous year (see figure 3).

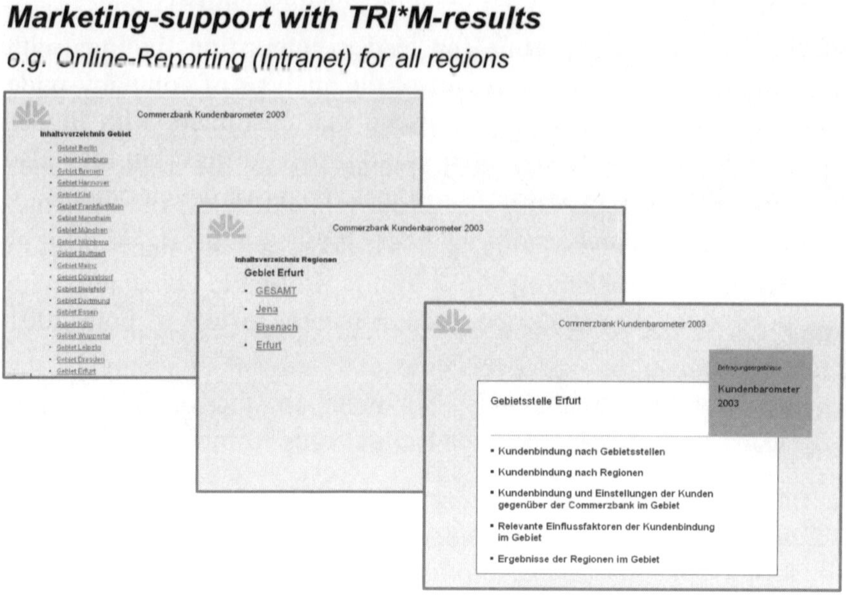

Fig. 3

These results include both, the TRI*M Index in comparison, as well as the 4 separate questions and the ratings for the most important performance-related aspects (which are typically the Motivators, and some standard aspects).

In the past (when the results were still split at branch-level) we had also attached a 'to-do list' to these reports, including suggestions and hints for measures to be implemented. However, as this proved to be a very demanding task in terms of monitoring, we chose to, by and large, discontinue this section; yet, this turned out not to be a sensible decision.

Many employees, particularly in operational units – although this might prove hard to believe – work in a more focussed manner, if they are in possession of a to-do list that they can adhere to. It may sound like an exaggeration to some, but based on our experience of day-to-day operations, this has become our certain and unmistakable conclusion; and it will probably prove to be true beyond the financial sector, that most operational personnel only implement what is provided to them in the form of a printed "instruction".

Although we still won't be able to realize, as strictly as necessary due to limited manpower, a consistent level of control of measures planned in relation to customer satisfaction; we nevertheless intend, to provide the above-mentioned documents to the regions once again, as well as establishing a controlling measure of sorts, through the us of so called "league tables," based on the main TRI*M scores.

But even in the absence of strict measures of controlling (in this context, in terms of control rather than directives), sales teams, particularly managers, have become markedly more aware of the fact, that investing in increasing customer satisfaction, also, eventually leads to increases in revenue (and thus to increased bonuses for themselves).

As already mentioned, the development of the main TRI*M scores will be more strictly monitored in the future as an annual overview; and thus, these scores will show most clearly, whether, or to what degree, measures have been successfully implemented, in the respective regions in question.

5.1.4 Future Plans

Data mining:

Besides monitoring customer retention, customer satisfaction and performance-related aspects, this year, we are planning to use the results of TRI*M more extensively, in order to analyse the behaviour of customers with respect to their retention and satisfaction; and use this, to facilitate our marketing and sales activities on both strategic as well as tactical and operational levels.

To this end, we have expanded the part of the survey conducted over the phone; that is, the "long version" of our questionnaire, by including a so-called VoC (Voice of the Customer) section. This supplementary section of the survey, which did not directly form an original part of TRI*M, aims to establish the customers dealings with Commerzbank on the one side, and our competitors on the other, with regard to their private financial affairs - over a specific period of time (within the past 4 to 6 weeks). It includes questions like:

Has the customer bought a product from us?

Has the customer bought a product from our competitors?

Has the customer cancelled products he/she held with us?

Has the customer cancelled products he/she held with our competitors?

Has the customer shifted a proportion of his/her assets to us?

Has the customer shifted a proportion of his/her assets away from us?

Has the customer been annoyed with us?

Has the customer complained about us?

How have we reacted to the complaint? etc.

Furthermore, we use this opportunity to attempt to establish whether the customer has had a consultation with one of our consultants in the recent past, and what action the customer has taken as a result. For example, we are interested to discover whether the customer has been actively approached by his consultant over the phone, and with what reaction this contact was met; in addition, to whether the customer has received advertising (direct mail) from us, and how this was reacted to.

While all the responses to these questions, are of interest to us if taken out of context; they also enable us to conduct far more revealing analyses, when they are put into the context of the relevant customer's satisfaction.

Through this process, we can gain a deeper insight into the question of whether, and particularly, which specific correlations exist, between specific methods of approaching customers, customer satisfaction as well as very specific reactions (such as product acquisition and cancellation).

Alternatively, we have the opportunity of examining the question of how dissatisfied customers, as opposed to very satisfied ones, react; with respect to the shifting around of assets, the acquisition of products from competitors, etc.

We want to use this initiative, in order to pursue opportunities in data mining and data matching processes, with greater determination than previously. Although, there is no doubt that satisfied customers are generally more loyal; and in the long term yield a higher level of revenue, it is still to be debated, as to the correlations between specific actions, customer satisfaction, the customers' reactions, and most importantly: the combinations which lead to the strongest degree of leverage.

Therefore, we can ask the question of, to what extent customers who have more frequent conversations with their consultants are more satisfied; and, whether conversations over the phone have the same effect as face-to-face conversations; and, what combination yields the highest probability of a product acquisition with our bank, or a shift of assets to our bank, taking place.

Moreover the correlation, of under which circumstances customers' tendencies to acquire products from our competitors are at their strongest or, preferably, at their weakest; are a very interesting aspect indeed; and its relationship to satisfaction, methods of approaching customers etc. are of major interest to us.

5.1.5 TRI*M Employee Commitment

Even though we have given for some years consideration to the possibility of supplementing the Customer TRI*M with an Employee TRI*M in accordance with the stakeholder concept; we have repeatedly postponed this step for a multitude of internal and external reasons; but as everyone knows, all's well that ends well, and so:

This year, for the first time, we will be conducting a satisfaction survey of all employees working in the retail banking sector, using the TRI*M Methodology. The topics covered will include the classic areas, such as the importance of, and satisfaction with: the workplace, salary, information, leadership etc. In addition, a so-called 'mirror image evaluation' section will be included. This mirror image evaluation, examines how the employees estimate the customers' evaluation, of their satisfaction with Commerzbank. By comparing these results to those from our customer satisfaction survey of this year, we will clearly be able to see where we rated ourselves too high, and where too low.

Additionally, the employee survey provides a scale similar to the TRI*M Index: the OCI (Organisational Commitment Index). This index is compiled from questions relating to satisfaction with the terms of employment, the likelihood of recommending the employer, the likelihood of re-applying, how colleagues' motivation is perceived, and an evaluation of performance in the marketplace.

The appeal of this approach, is that just like our customer TRI*M, we are able to use a single score for internal and external benchmarking.

An exiting question from our perspective how do the regional TRI*M scores compare to the OCI?

These two steps form part of our market research using TRI*M, and they are specifically geared towards facilitating customer loyalty and increases in revenue. We are convinced that they will help us to improve, even more.

6 The Czech Beer Market: A Brief Introduction – Understanding Consumers and Customer Needs

Zuzana Heleyová

Czech beer and Czech culture seem to go together very well. When asked, consumers themselves (spontaneously) mention beer as being very much a part of Czech culture. The beer market in the Czech Republic has a number of characteristics which make it unique in comparison with other beer markets globally.

The average per capita consumption of beer in the Czech Republic occupies the first place on a global scale at about 160 litres per year. This consumption has stayed quite level in recent years. Despite this high number, the beer market (from the product point of view) does not offer a very colourful picture. Beer consumption is covered almost completely by domestic brands - imports account for only about one per cent. About 98% of the overall domestic production is covered by Pilsner-style lager; the other 2% is dark beer variants and speciality beers. Another feature differentiating the Czech beer market from other strong beer markets is the trend in the package ratio development: due to a relatively lower price premium when comparing draught and packaged beer (which goes hand in hand with the high density of pubs, restaurants and other places for on-trade consumption), the share of draught beer has grown in recent years at the expense of packaged beer, currently reaching over 54% of the total domestic market.

Apart from channel consolidation (growing on-trade accompanied by a better-profiled retail universe), the dynamics of the overall market in recent years have not been so great. Due to the quite traditional or even conservative approach of beer drinkers to "their beer", the changes are only minor and do not result in dramatic or substantial movement in the market. It should therefore be obvious for every beer producer that keeping or further improving the position reached on the market is a task which requires an in-depth understanding of the market, good insight into consumers' and customers' needs, their habits, preferences and behaviour, and for them to excel in operational performance in order to implement the potential changes and adjustments in real life.

Plensky Pradzdroj, as a company that has retained its position for several years with the highest share in the Czech beer market, is well aware of the need to understand the market in detail, from different perspectives. One of the areas where it has felt it has had a lack of in-depth knowledge in recent years is the on-trade channel. Before dealing with this problem, it is first worth describing this particular channel in a little more detail.

On-Trade and Off-Trade Channels

As with many other FMCG (Fast Moving Consumer Goods) categories, the off-trade channel (mainly the retail market) is quite straightforward when producers communicate with consumers through the brand - through its product characteristics, price, place-ment and promotional activities. More-over, the performance in the off-trade channel can be measured from different angles via a set of retail audit methodologies, which have had growing validity in recent years.

On the other hand, the communication with the consumer on-trade is less simplistic and straightforward. The difference is perhaps well described by the traditional belief of many beer lovers:"The brewery produces the beer, but it is the barman who creates it".

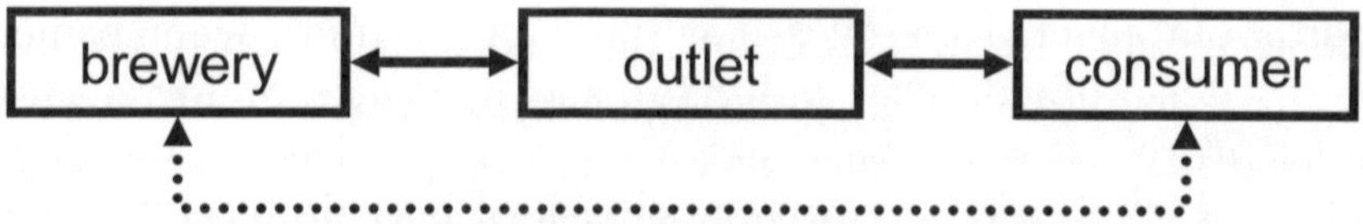

Fig. 1: Communication to Consumers: Outlets Own the Brewery's Core Consumers

The density of on-trade outlets in the Czech market is relatively high (about 3.5 on-trade outlets per 1000 inhabitants); the natural question that arises is therefore the need to understand what attracts consumers to the most popular pubs: what really matters when choosing a pub for the next beer, which details are appreciated and which are less relevant, and to what extent the selection of the pub is influenced by the brand available, the price, etc.

To move ahead in understanding this area of consumer behaviour we (PPAS) decided to apply the TRI*M Methodology in several areas of our work.

1st Step: Better Understanding the Consumer's View

We first applied TRI*M Methodology in 2003 when we used this approach for evaluating the retention of on-trade beer drinkers, in particular on-trade outlets. Due to the quite high requirements of the study, we proceeded in regional waves. In one year we monitored a small panel of outlets in each particular sales region and afterwards we shared the results at internal workshops with S&D teams. The workshops quickly helped us to gain feedback for further steps and make improvements in the study. Also, direct discussion between the research team (research agency) and the key users of the results about the information gained from the trade was highly useful. It helped break in the barriers between the "theoretical" knowledge of the research agency and the "real life" experiences of the sales force. It was not possible to avoid high emotions sometimes - mainly when the results may not have been fully in line with users' expectations. Still, the strength of the results allowed open discussion that helped us to reach mutual agreement at the end of each workshop.

The accumulated results from this first "consumer" part of the project gave us quite a clear overall picture of the market. The accumulated map of the market gave us evidence of how emotionally intense the connection between consumers and the pub can be. In more detail, some of the best-evaluated outlets were particularly well rated (as above-average motivators) in the area of service (including clean tablecloths, a variety of tables (for bigger groups), friendliness and willingness of the personnel, and letting the guests finish after closing hours). The perceived quality and impor-tance of beer differed according to the type of outlet: while in some places the beer itself was almost in the savings area (even with high volumes of it drunk at the pub) we discovered several types of outlets where the role of the beer was very important, including the beer brand itself.

2nd Step: Better Understanding the Customer's View

The natural continuation, after positive acceptance of the TRI*M result during the first year, was to focus on the mutual relationship between the supplier and customer. We started with a more-or-less standard approach. To agree with the list of characteristics monitored we initiated an internal workshop involving the key people responsible. We followed this with qualitative research with pub managers and sales reps, then another internal workshop, collection of feedback, fine-tuning the questionnaire, etc. Neverthe-less we faced another difficult task - how to define the sample structure that would actually deliver us actionable results. To base our decision on as strong information as possible, we decided to undertake another preparatory step in the whole project and used phone interviews for measuring the TRI*M Index only amongst a selected sub-sample of our on-trade customers. Several interesting aspects were learnt at this stage of the study. In first place was the extremely positive factor that the response rate reached about 70% of the sample used. The final results gave us clear evidence that the beer market in the Czech Republic is a "good-relationship" market. More precisely:

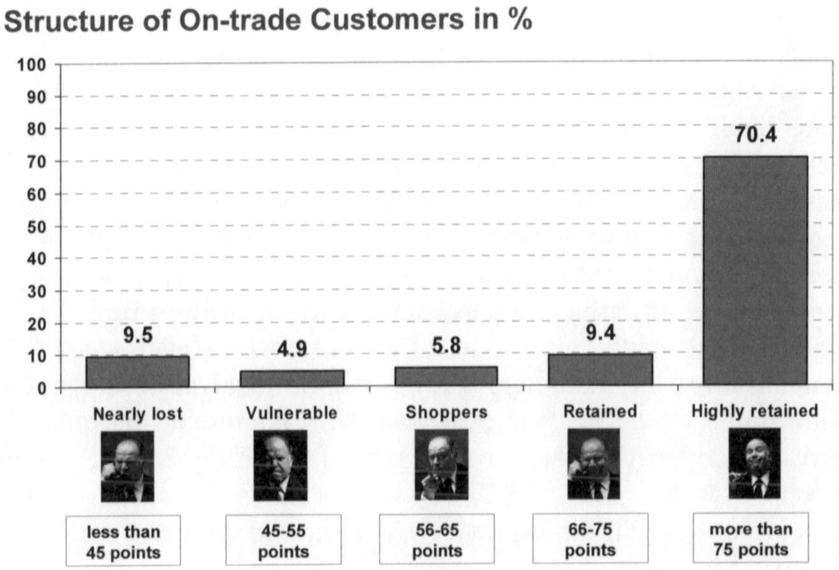

Fig. 2: Customer Structure

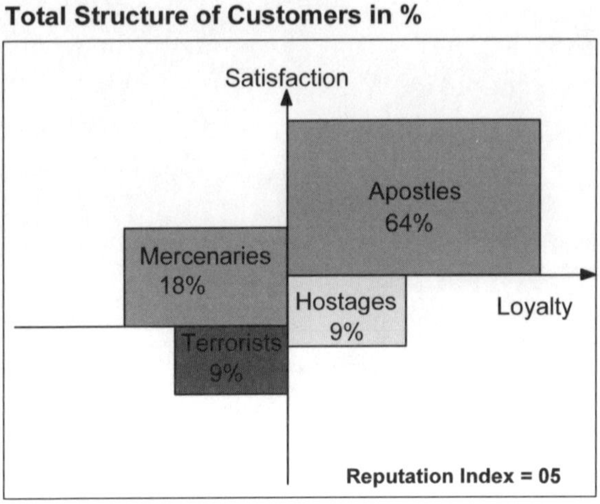

*Fig. 3: TRI*M Segments in Total*

Despite the very good retention overall amongst on-trade customers, we continued the study with detailed interviews of 700 customers across all regions, including some outlets with competitor brands on tap as well. For revealing the key issues of cooperation with our customers, we decided to increase the proportion of terrorists, mercenaries and hostages at the expense of apostles in the sample (a fair split of each segment amongst our customers). The final results allowed us to compare groups of long-term customers, multi-brand customers and recent switchers. When thinking about the sample structure, one of the working hypotheses was to include quite a high share of multi-brand outlets into the study. Some members of the team expected the customers who dealt with different beer suppliers at the same time to be the best experts in comparing our and our competitors' performance, and our weak and strong sides. The final agreement was to include only a quarter of the multi-branded outlets in the sample. Still, the results collected in this subgroup were very surprising for us.

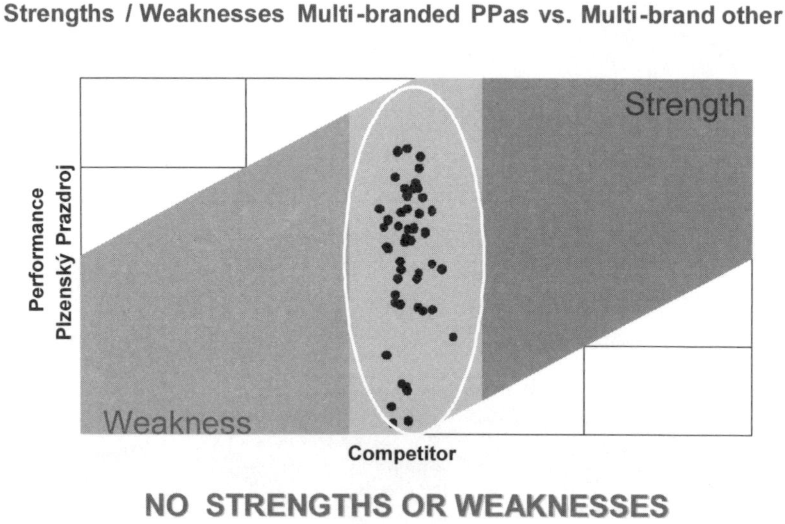

Fig. 4: Comparison of Competitive Advantages Between Multi-Brand Outlets

Another thing learnt from the study was the important role of time in people's evaluation of both the positive and negative aspects of mutual cooperation. It was good that some (at first glance) less popular principles applied from us for our customers (mainly in the area of very strict conditions of cooperation) was finally accepted and rated on an average level. On the other hand, amongst some long-term customers the excellent quality of all the brands in our portfolio moved to the hygienics area - customers had simply got used to it and took it for granted.

As in the previous year, except for the summary presentation given at senior management levels, to make the S&D teams familiar with the results, we prepared several "country region" workshops where results from a particular region were shared and discussed.

Overall, this type of study was well accepted by the S&D team, and was based on their requirements. This autumn we will be initiating the next part of the detailed TRI*M study (another 900 outlets). We believe that by connecting both these waves of the study we can get sufficiently reliable information on each sales region.

Due to difficulties with defining the representative sample, the TRI*M Index and TRI*M Segment information from these detailed studies play only a secondary role. Nevertheless, we plan to repeat the phone measurement of the TRI*M Index on a yearly basis. We expect that by connecting these two types of approaches (detailed diagnostics on a smaller sample and reliable measurement of the TRI*M Index and segments) we can obtain suitable information for tactics and strategy for customer service adjustments; and evaluating changes in company performance in the market (as an important part of the company scorecards).

Next Steps

We are now using the TRI*M Tools in different types of studies. Next year we envisage to implement the positive experiences from the on-trade channel on the Czech market onto the Slovak market as well. We are applying for the TRI*M Reputation Manager for measuring perceptions of the company's reputation in the Czech Republic, and again a similar study will follow on the Slovak market in the near future. We applied the TRI*M Grid with very good results in evaluating a newly launched product (Frisco) on the Czech market, amongst different subgroups of the target audience.

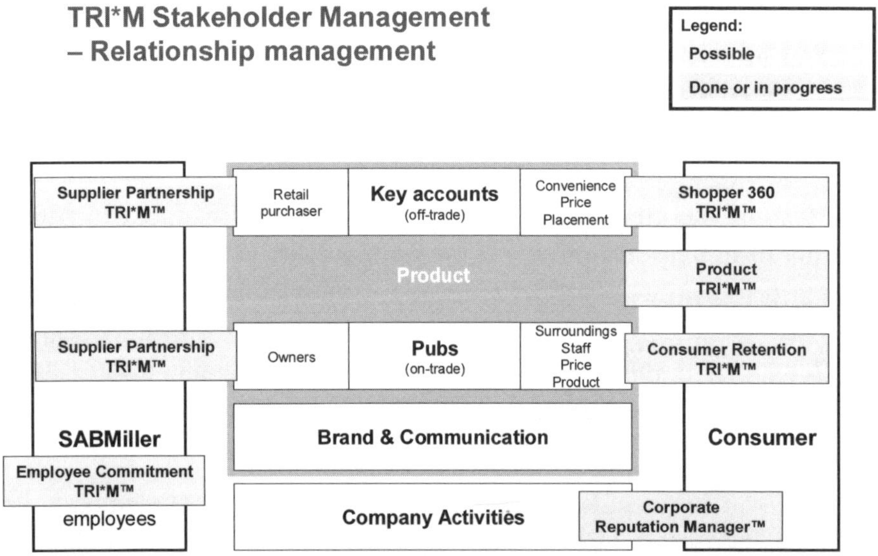

*Fig. 5: The TRI*M Product Has Different Modules that Help to Manage Any Mutual Relationship Related to the Company: Currently Used TRI*M + Identification of the TRI*M Applications in the Next Period*

7 Measuring and Monitoring Stakeholder Relationships: Using TRI*M as an Innovative Tool for Corporate Communication

Susanne O'Gorman, Peter Pirner

The importance of corporate communication for the management of stakeholder relationships is no longer a matter of controversy. This article demonstrates firstly (using the example of customer loyalty) how the communication between a company and individual groups of stakeholders can be analysed with the help of TRI*M Customer Retention and which options are available to companies as a way of dealing with this. Secondly, it shows how integrated and comprehensive control of corporate communication is rendered possible using TRI*M Corporate Reputation Manager.

7.1 The Importance of Communication for the Management of Stakeholder Relationships

Communication is a necessary prerequisite for corporate success (cf. Pfannenberg 2004) and as such is at the same time the foundation of stakeholder relationships within a company: employees, customers, suppliers, retailers, shareholders, the general public. The relationship to these stakeholder groups is characterised not only by the exchange of benefits (products and services in return for payment) but also at least equally strongly by communication. The manner in which communication takes place with the groups of stakeholders is by definition crucial to the success of a company. As a result the way in which this communication is managed becomes a central function of the management. At the same time communication in modern stakeholder management also has to take into account the stakeholders' communication with one another ("what our customers are talking about").

Frequently, however, insufficient attention is paid to this multi-dimensionality of communication in stakeholder relationships. In many cases companies have a number of different performance indicators (compliance with quality standards, number of complaints, technical availability of hotlines, etc.) but seldom regard themselves as being in a position to measure the factor of "communication". It is true that companies know how great their expenditure is for PR and advertising, but they are seldom clear about how well their sales department communicates with customers or how a complaints hotline can be responsive to customer needs – and as a result they are foregoing essential information for managing the business. Overall this frequently results in it becoming impossible to syste-matically evaluate the targeted communication with stakeholders when the management makes decisions as an entrepreneurial option and thus also ultimately to it not being possible to manage this efficiently.

7.2 Communication with Individual Stakeholder Groups – Taking TRI*M Customer Retention as an Example

TRI*M (= Measuring, Managing, Monitoring) was developed at the beginning of the 1990s and since that time has been successfully implemented in more than 900 companies worldwide. TRI*M Systematics permits the analysis of all stakeholder groups using comparable, standardised performance indicators and thus enables this information to be integrated into the Balanced Scorecard: as well as measuring customer retention using TRI*M Customer Retention, TRI*M also, for example, facilitates analysis of employee commitment (TRI*M Employee Commitment), measurement of the strength of the management (TRI*M Management Evaluation) and process-oriented measurement of the internal service quality of a company (TRI*M Internal Service Quality).

7.3 The TRI*M Index

The TRI*M Index is a performance indicator for measuring the status quo of a stakeholder relationship – whether it be the intensity of customer retention or, for example, the commitment of the employees. This "one number tool" consists (in our example of customer loyalty) of four questions which reflect the different aspects of the stakeholder relationship: the overall performance of the company, the recommendation of the company to others, the repurchasing of products / services and the competitive advantage of a company. An index value of 70 stands for a high level of intensity of customer loyalty, whilst an index value of 40 implies that the company has not succeeded in creating real customer retention. In terms of corporate communication, the level of the TRI*M Index gives information about possible deficiencies in communication with stakeholder groups. In addition, the TRI*M Index also facilitates external benchmarking which can be carried out by country, region or sector. Here TRI*M falls back on a database with over 7,000 customer studies and more than 10 million interviews and enables companies not only to compare themselves with the average in their sector but also gives information about the level of customer retention for example, in the top 10% and bottom 10% of companies.

	Bottom 10%	Bottom 33%	Average	Top 33%	Top 10%
Worldwide	51	65	**71**	78	89
Western Europe	48	62	**68**	74	86
US	59	71	**75**	82	90
Asia	50	62	**67**	73	86

Source: TRI*M Benchmarking Database 2004

*Fig. 1: TRI*M Index Benchmarking / Customer Retention According to Regions*

7.4 TRI*M Typology and Market Resistance Value

It is generally known that customers speak more frequently about the bad experiences than about the positive experiences that they have had with a company: angry customers ("Terrorists") speak more than three times as frequently about their bad experiences than satisfied customers ("Apostles") speak about a positive experience. "Terrorists" is a label given to dissatisfied customers who show little loyalty and who because of their negative word-of-mouth can seriously damage a company. "Apostles" on the other hand are extremely satisfied and loyal customers who recommend the company to other people and thus contribute to a positive mood in the market. Both types of customers are part of the TRI*M Typology whose proportions are determined mathematically from answers to the four TRI*M Index Questions (cf. also Huber/ Scharioth 2002: 56; Jones/Sasser 1995).

*Fig. 2: TRI*M Typology of Customer Experience*

Thus for there to be a "balanced" mood on the market, ten very satisfied customers are necessary to offset three dissatisfied cu stomers. The market resistance value reproduces this mood on the market:

$$\frac{\text{Share of Terrorists} \times 10}{\text{Share of Apostles} \times 3} = \text{Market Resistance Ratio}$$

Example for the minimum target

$$\frac{15\% \times 10}{50\% \times 3} = \frac{150}{150} = 1$$

Fig. 3: Market Resistance Ratio

If the market resistance value is < 1, then more positive experiences than negative ones are being passed on. If the market resistance value is > 1, then the negative experiences are clearly prevailing. If there is little market resistance, the company can use the high level of customer satisfaction offensively and emphasise this as strength in its communications with the stakeholders. If the market resistance is negative, then in the first instance the company must again create confidence among the stakeholders by good performances and focus the communication on those aspects which (despite negative experiences) are still being rated as good from the customers' point of view.

7.5 TRI*M Grid

In order to manage communication efficiently, a company has to know which products and services are important for the stakeholders. Information about this is shown with the help of the TRI*M Grid (cf. fig. 4).

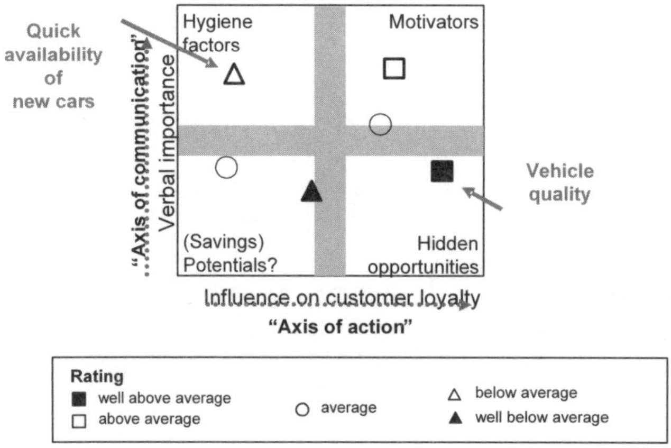

*Fig. 4: TRI*M Grid: An Example from the Automobile Market*

With its simple graphics tools the TRI*M Grid gives clear-cut answers to three pivotal questions (cf. Scharioth/Pirner 1999: 332ff).

1. What aspects do the stakeholders talk about particularly frequently? (Position on the axis of communication)
2. How is the company rated in these aspects? (Symbols showing the Quality element)
3. Which of these aspects actually have an influence on loyalty to a company? (Position on the axis of action)

The positioning within the TRI*M Grid gives an indication of how corporate communication can be managed. In the example shown here, vehicle quality has a high level of influence on customer loyalty and at the same time the customers are extremely satisfied with the quality achieved. But on the axis of communication it can be seen that the customers speak significantly more frequently of other aspects. Therefore vehicle quality ought to be communicated more offensively and more clearly in order to become a real motivator for customer loyalty. On the other hand, in this example customer satisfaction with the availability of new cars is below average – this weakness has already got around in the market and is strongly anchored in the consciousness of customers. Here the focus of the company's actions must be on improving the delivery process. So long as no improvement takes place here from the customers' point of view, this aspect needs to be dealt with rather more defensively in corporate communications.

For each aspect that is investigated the TRI*M Grid gives concrete pointers towards a sensible communications strategy as regards to the customers. As a result, communication measures can be developed in a targeted manner and implemented where they achieve the greatest effect.

Comprehensive control of corporate communication using the TRI*M Corporate Reputation Manager.

The advantages of a good reputation for commercial success are beyond dispute in theory and practice. A company with an outstanding reputation achieves higher prices even in markets where the competition is intense, is a motivating environment for achievers within the company, is more attractive for new employees ("high potentials") and forms an effective barrier against new competitors entering the market.

But what makes for a good Corporate Reputation? How can it be influenced? And what is the framework of reference which should form the basis of how it can be controlled efficiently?

Corporate Reputation is the emotional and rational assessment of a company by its stakeholders. This assessment can be influenced by active, targeted corporate communication. Each item of communication that is addressed to a stakeholder group also has at the same time an effect – directly or indirectly – on other stakeholders. News about an improvement in a company's financial situation is not only received positively by investors but also has an effect on employees: for example, with regard to security of employment. At the same time a company's customers and employees themselves have a considerable effect on the building up of its reputation, for to a great extent recommendations and experiences "at first hand" come across as credible. They can even interfere with corporate communication and thus lead to desirable or undesirable side effects.

The TRI*M Corporate Reputation Index determines whether and (if yes) in which stakeholder group the company's reputation is endangered. The indicator is comparable for all groups. Insights from existing theoretical approaches and assured results from a large number of practical market research projects were combined in the TRI*M Corporate Reputation Manager. In less than three years since 2002 it has already proved itself as a tool for comprehensive analysis and management in more than 30 customer projects worldwide. On the basis of five individual questions, the TRI*M Corporate Reputation Index summarises the central rational and emotional aspects which are equally relevant to all stakeholders in the form of a measured value. It then implies that a company has a very good reputation if the stakeholders are of the opinion that

- the company generally has a good reputation among the general public
- it is appealing to the respondent (Emotional Attractiveness 1)
- they can trust the company (Emotional Attractiveness 2)

- the products and services are of high quality (Attractiveness as a result of Competence 1), and
- the company is commercially successful (Attractiveness as a result of Competence 2).

The five partial indicators selected have proved themselves with different stakeholder groups and in over 40 countries. According to this, the concepts of emotional attractiveness and attractiveness as a result of competence also apply cross-culturally. On the basis of the TRI*M Benchmarking Database, regional peculiarities in the manner of responding can be taken into account in the interpretation of the results.

With the TRI*M Corporate Reputation Index the interrelationships between good reputation and the behaviour of individual stakeholders can be proven: in several studies it was observed that the index value of customers was significantly higher than that of people who were not customers of the company – an indicator of the positive effect of a good reputation in the opening up of sales markets. Using the TRI*M Reputation Index it was also possible to contextualise the tendency to make applications to a particular company.

7.6 A Holistic View Using Reputation Radar

TRI*M Corporate Reputation Radar combines the results of the Reputation Index for all stakeholders. As a result it is possible to get a differentiated 360° view of all the stakeholders that are relevant to the company – customers, suppliers, employees, investors. The Radar detects very quickly whether the level of reputation is homogeneous or whether individual groups of stakeholders show lower values than others. This would then point to the fact that the communication strategy for this group must be looked into more closely and that the causes of the inferior reputation values need to be established.

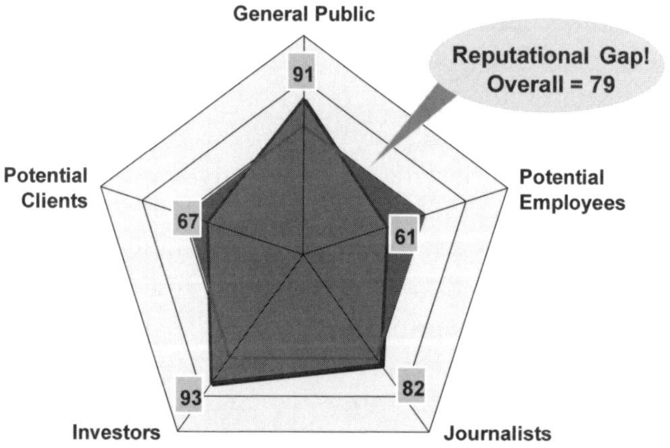

*Fig. 5: TRI*M Corporate Reputation Radar*

The Benchmarking Database helps in the recognition of "normal" differences in the levels between the stakeholders. In this database 10 stakeholder groups are identified and systematically recorded. As experience with the project grows, the insights previously gained for customers, non-customers and employees are also extended towards other stakeholders. In customer projects which have already been carried out, up to five stakeholder groups have been surveyed at the same time. The flexibility in adapting the system to the actual corporate situation and the possibility of extending the frame of reference within the time limit are yet more reasons for the high level of acceptance of the process in practice.

7.7 Derivation of the New Measures on the Basis of the TRI*M Grid

The TRI*M System Grid Analysis makes it possible to identify the driving force behind the reputation and to derive appropriate communication strategies. Even when setting up the system it is necessary to include central aspects of the company's image which have regularly been the subject of corporate communication (core values). In addition, other potential driving forces behind the company's reputation which are well-established but which may not have been investigated up to now should be integrated, e.g. an ethical behaviour, quality of management, etc. Finally, starting from this basis set of 20 – 30 reputation drivers which is comparable across all stakeholders, another 5 – 10 specific driving forces should be surveyed for each stakeholder group. This increases the practical benefits of the tool enormously.

The open statistical analysis model used enables one to reconcile the driving force analyses with the experiences of the stakeholders in the best possible way. By determining the common ground among all the stakeholders, the core values of the company for the overall strategy can be scrutinised and optimised. At the same time, synergy potentials can be recognised in the way things are presented to the outside world and made use of in proactive reputation management.

Literature

Huber, Margit/Scharioth, Joachim (2002): Balanced Scorecard als Werkzeug für den Controller, in: Der Controllingberater, Volume 1, 2002, pp. 43-62.

Jones, Thomas O./W. Earl Sasser (1995): Why satisfied customers defect, in: Harvard Business Review (November/December), pp. 88-99.

Pfannenberg, Jörg (2004): Das Projekt "Wertschöpfung durch Kommunikation". Thesis on the strategic control of communications in companies and institutions, Bonn.

Scharioth, Joachim/Pirner, Peter (1999): TRI*M - Messung der Kundenbindung im Dienste des Stakeholdermanagements, in: Herrmann, A./Jasny, R./Vetter, I. (Ed.): Kundenorientierung von Banken. Strategien für Kundennähe und effektives Beziehungsmanagement, Frankfurt am Main 1999, pp. 323-347.

8 Customer Satisfaction and Retention Improves with Six Sigma

Lynnette Leathers

8.1 Background

CHEP has reported three year revenue results with a compound annual growth rate (CAGR) of 10% for the years ending 2005 stated in constant currency terms. During the same three consecutive years CHEP has improved Customer Satisfaction and Loyalty between two and three percentage points. As measured with the TNS TRI*M methodology this translates to approximately two index points per annum. Although all variables can not be isolated; this indicates that if you improve Customer Satisfaction and Loyalty by at least two percentage points, per year revenue is likely to increase by 10%.

CHEP is a division of Brambles Group, which is a leading Industrial Service provider that operates in almost 50 countries across six continents and employs approximately 28,000 people. The group's other major on-going business is Recall, which provides secure storage, access, retrieval and tracking of important information. Brambles' global headquarters are in Sydney, Australia, and the group maintains corporate offices in Sydney, London, and Atlanta. Headquarters of the major businesses are in Orlando, USA (CHEP Americas), Weybridge, England (CHEP Europe), and Atlanta, USA (Recall).

The companies have some 100,000 private and institutional shareholders. Brambles posted revenue of over A$8 billion (approximately US$6 billion) for Fiscal Year 2005.

CHEP EBITA represents more than 50% of the Brambles business portfolio and has global headquarters in Orlando, Florida. CHEP is the global leader in pallet and container pooling services, serving customers in a wide range of industrial and retail supply chains, including consumer goods, fruit and vegetable, meat, home improvement, beverage, raw materials, petro-chemical and automotive industries.

CHEP partners with raw materials and ingredients suppliers, manufacturers, growers, transporters, distributors and retailers to move their products through the supply chain, improving efficiencies, reducing costs and meeting their customers' needs. This enables CHEP's customers to reduce the need for capital expenditures and concentrate on their core business competencies.

CHEP manages the daily movement of over 280 million pallets and containers from a global network of over 440 service centers in 42 countries. With more than 300,000 customers worldwide, CHEP's customers are global giants such as Procter & Gamble, SYSCO, Carrefour, Kellogg's, ESSO, Shell, Woolworths, Kraft, Nestle, Lion Nathan, The Home Depot, Tesco, Unilever, Hewlett Packard, Ford and GM, "Handling the World's Most Important Products... Everyday."

HOW POOLING WORKS

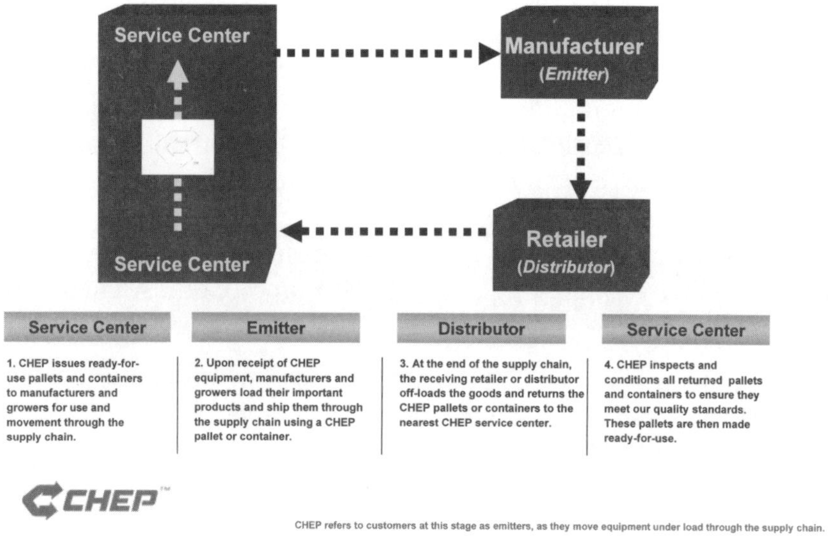

Fig. 1

CHEP™

Fig. 2

In its simplest form, pallet and container pooling is the shared use of CHEP STANDARD pallets and containers by multiple customers or users. Pallet and container pooling is a strategic business option for companies that wish to improve their day-to-day supply chain operations and reduce their capital expenditures.

Commitment to Customer Satisfaction and Loyalty

CHEP globally was experiencing year on year double-digit growth by expanding business with existing customers, expanding into new countries, enhancing products and services, and adding customers. However, there was rapid growth in some markets and entrenchment in other markets. The level of competition varies by country and product. Due to the fast growth, some infrastructure issues need to be addressed to support the business. It was important to determine a benchmark for customers in each market to identify key risks in the business and clearly determine which markets were more successful and would allow the opportunity to share best practices across markets. In addition, the business model that CHEP utilizes may vary by market. Therefore, there is variation in business models, business processes, product dimensions, the number of competitors, the maturity of the CHEP pooling system in the market, and the emerging nature of some markets themselves (i.e, Central Europe, Asia, and Latin America). A common measurement and language were needed to measure customer satisfaction, customer loyalty (retention), determine opportunities to improve, and establish best practices.

CHEP chose TNS as a research provider and utilizes the TRI*M Methodology to meet the business needs. This is a significant commitment for a Business to Business (B2B) company. Large consumer package goods companies typically invest in customer satisfaction research to a much greater extent than B2B companies. In fact, assuming that B2B companies met the average B2B investment it would still be less than .02% of revenues[1]. A benchmark TRI*M study was completed across all businesses. Subsequently, the largest markets are measured on an annual basis (USA, Europe, and Asia Pacific) and the developing markets are measured on a biennial basis.

The CHEP survey includes 30-40 attributes which are critical to quality (CTQs) that were developed by obtaining qualitative feedback from customers and employees. The attributes are reviewed and refined each year based on the verbatim responses of Customers. The attributes utilized by CHEP are related to pallet and container management, customer focus and relationship, responsiveness and quality of staff, invoicing and transactions, and value. The results of the TRI*M surveys have been essential in helping the company focus on opportunities to improve that are important and relevant to the customer, which are classified as "Motivators" in the TRI*M Prioritization Grids. CHEP made a number of business changes in markets that were monitored by the annual TRI*M survey. The first step is to be aware of issues that impact customers and the relative importance of these issues to the overall satisfaction and ultimately retention of a customer. There are two challenges in communicating across a broad range of markets. The first is to

---

[1] TNS London estimate of B2B spend on customer satisfaction research in 2005.

communicate in a way that would be a call to action for each market. This involves educating a business to business company on the research methodology and clearly bringing the voice of the customer into the decision making process. In addition to the attributes that are key to the CHEP business, the survey has two open-ended questions that allow the customers to provide feedback in their own words to CHEP. This has been beneficial to bringing the voice of the customer (VOC) into the business.

One of the open-ended questions is an unaided question to customers who did not rate CHEP performance as Excellent or Very Good (Top 2 box). The customers are asked what CHEP could do to be rated excellent or very good. The other question involves problems. If a customer called the company in the last 12 months with a problem, what was the problem and was it resolved to your satisfaction? There is a correlation with problem resolution and customer satisfaction. If there is a reduction in the number of problems and an increase in the percentage of problems resolved satisfactorily, the probability of increasing the TRI*M Index improves. Often improvements are made or projects developed on the basis of these answers, which are coded and provided by country. Successful projects and improvements are then used to establish best practices.

There are many diverse markets with varying opportunities and abilities to improve. Therefore, some markets are improving while others remain flat or declining, even when it is identified that the Index should increase to be more consistent with the CHEP Global Business Index. This was one reason the company adopted the Six Sigma methodology commonly used by notable companies like Motorola[2], GE, Honeywell, and Allied Signal.

Six Sigma

Six Sigma is an organized and rigorous methodology for the continuous improvement of all business processes – Process, Variation, and Customer.

Six Sigma is a statistical concept that represents the amount of variation present in a process relative to customer requirements or

---

[2] Motorola holds the Six Sigma trademark for the Six Sigma Methodology.

specifications. When a process operates at the six sigma level, the variation is so small that the resulting products and services are 99.9997% defect free.

The term Six Sigma also refers to a business philosophy of focusing on continuous improvement by understanding customers' needs, analyzing business processes, and instituting proper measurement methods. The goal is to get as close to six standard deviations between the mean and the nearest specification limit) in any process. At CHEP this can be a manufacturing or a transactional process or a process for a product or service.

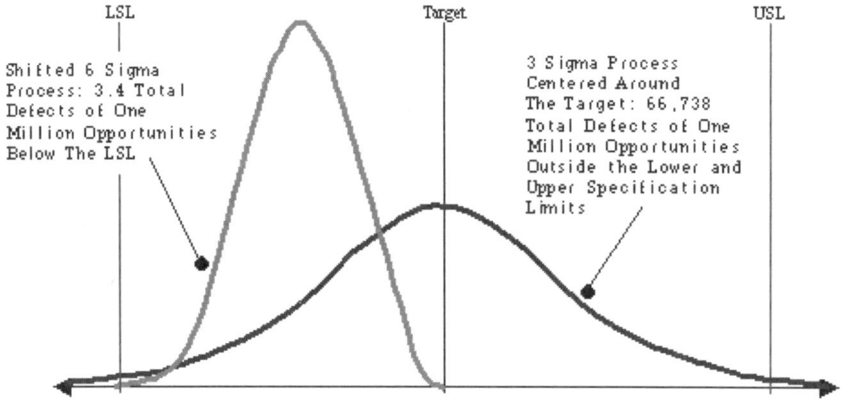

Fig. 3

A process sigma may mean its standard deviation, which is a measurement of variability or its capability to operate within the specifications. As the process sigma value increases from zero to six, the variation of the process around the mean value decreases. With a high enough value of process sigma, the process approaches zero variation and is known as 'zero defects.' An important concept is that the Defects Per Million of Opportunities (DPMO) is a measure in terms of sigma and quality levels (specifications).

Sigma Level	**DPMO**	**% In Specification**
2	**308,500**	**69.1**
3	**66,800**	**93.3**
4	**6,200**	**99.4**
5	**233**	**99.98**
6	**3.4**	**99.9997**

Fig. 4

A commonly used example of the difference between 99% quality (3.8 sigma) and 99.9997% quality (6 sigma) is the difference between 200,000 wrong drug prescriptions each year and 68 wrong drug prescriptions per year.

The Six Sigma process is to build a culture that is committed to excellence, which will benefit all stakeholders: Customers, Stockholders, and Employees. The methodology is considered by many to be a tool box to provide employees with the tools to be able to solve the problems of corporations. This empowers employees to directly impact customer satisfaction and loyalty; and therefore, improve the bottom line. Within the "tool box" are common definitions, project management and statistical methods to drive this data driven approach.

The process begins with understanding and measuring customer needs and building a project charter. The DMAIC model provides a disciplined approach of project management and is considered to be essential to the Six Sigma methodology. It provides a project framework, a common language, and prevents skipping critical process steps.

The DMAIC model consists of the following basic steps:

1) Define the project.

2) Measure the current situation.

3) Analyze to identify causes.

4) Improve.

5) Control.

Within each of these steps there is an opportunity to use statistical and project management methods to progress the project.

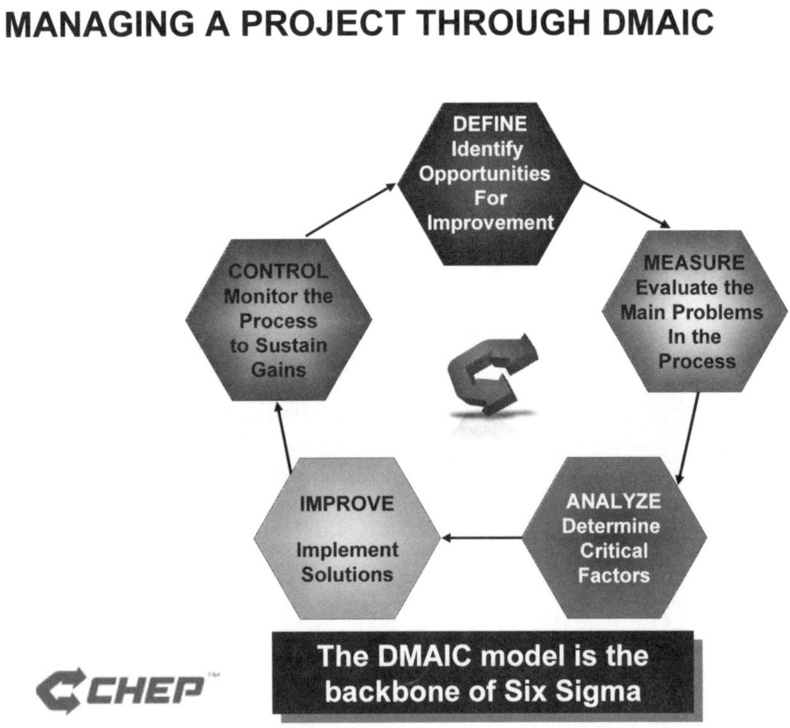

Fig. 5

If you decrease variation (by improving quality) the end result is greater customer satisfaction and lower costs[3]. Operational and manufacturing processes traditionally benefit from Six Sigma improvement. “Hard" discrete data can be counted and expressed as ratios. "Soft" data (opinions, attitudes, satisfaction) can also have statistical process controls applied if the appropriate data is avail-

[3] Michael D. Johnson and Anders Gustafsson, Improving Customer Satisfaction, Loyalty, and Profit, p.101, (Jossey - Bass Inc., 2000)

able. Market research provides quantitative data to what have traditionally been less definable processes. Examples are customer service processes and problem resolution processes.

The argument can be made that Market Research is the most sensible function for Six Sigma to reside provided you consider that typically all processes exist to deliver seamless service and value to customers. Therefore, the link between market research and stringent quantitative as well as qualitative feedback to the process provides additional opportunities to apply business process (Six Sigma).

Precursors to Six Sigma, such as, Edward Demming's Total Quality Management (TQM) theory focus on tangible quality. The arguable difference between TQM and Six Sigma is that business criteria must be applied to the decision. Improving quality may not be the best use of resources and the relative return may be small. Therefore, it is important to recognize the relevance of quality or any other dimension is not mutually exclusive of other business criteria.

CHEP Canada TRI*M Six Sigma Case Study

CHEP Canada has a TRI*M Index in top tertile of the TNS database. CHEP Canada began an annual Six Sigma Workshop to drive continuous improvement in the business. The workshop was facilitated by Market Research and two Six Sigma Blackbelts. It is important to note that the process has support of the senior leadership in CHEP Canada, including the president of the company[4]. The appropriate areas of focus were developed utilizing the DMAIC model and Pareto charts were prepared prior to the 2-day workshop. The Six Sigma projects are based on the TRI*M survey results. The workshop kicks off with a Customer Satisfaction presentation. The team members were people who had accountability in the business (not selected by title, included all levels - front line employee to VP) and cross functional representation.

---

[4] Mike Dimond, President CHEP Canada; Travis Ratnam, Six Sigma Black Belt; Jeff Doman, Six Sigma Black Belt; Lynnette Leathers, Head of CHEP Global Market Research, Six Sigma Green Belt.

Each of 4-5 groups was assigned a six sigma project. During the 2 days critical, key milestones and the deliverables were required at time intervals. The workshop goal was to complete as much of the project as possible during the workshop. At the end of the first day of the workshop, each team presented their project, and the top six sigma projects were agreed upon by management and resourced on the second day.

The first workshop (2003) served as a benchmark from which the Six Sigma projects were resourced to impact key attributes that would affect overall satisfaction and ultimately the TRI*M Index. The next annual Customer Satisfaction Survey and TRI*M Index was completed in 2004, and a 4 index point improvement was recorded. This is significant at a 95% confidence level. In addition, CHEP Canada indexes in the top tertile of the TNS database. Further analysis was conducted to determine if the Six Sigma process influenced the TRI*M index improvement.

TRI*M Six Sigma Validation for CHEP CANADA CASE STUDY

Measuring, Managing and Monitoring quality is a common and well-known management practice in the context of manufacturing processes. But measuring sales and service processes of non-manufacturing businesses and units is not because "Defects" come in all shapes and sizes. Measuring the quality of such processes becomes a complex task. In sales and service organizations – like CHEP – value is created when the business interacts with the customer. If such organizations are going to achieve sustainable growth and profitability the customer-business interface must be managed with great care. Customers define the quality of the business.

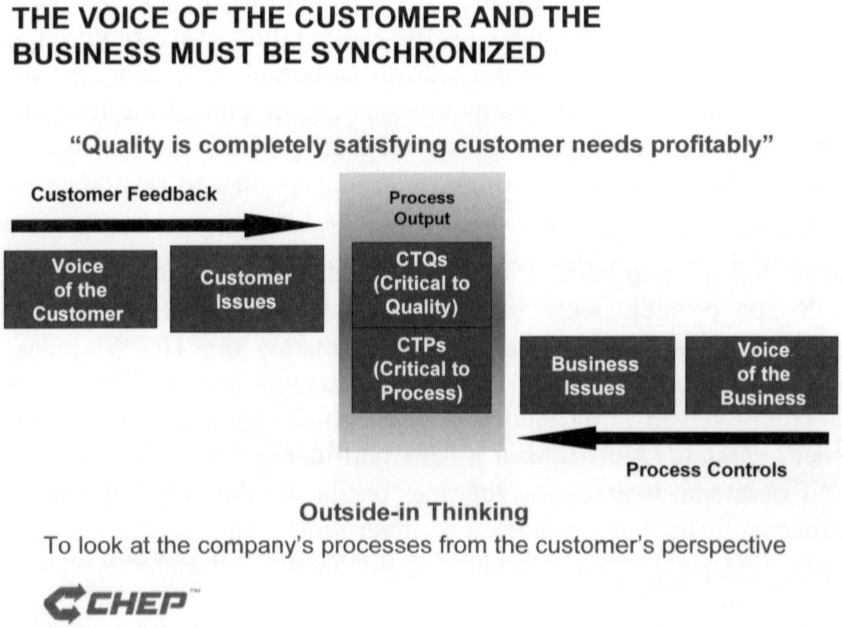

Fig. 6

Business Excellence requires the organization to look at the processes from a customer's perspective. In other words, the company must look at its processes from the outside-in. The TRI*M Six Sigma Case Study provides CHEP Canada with the customer's view of its individual service processes. TRI*M measures the Voice of the Customer in a standardized and consistent way and provides robust and comparable information over time. The survey data are translated into actionable insights for CHEP Canada.

The process of turning attitudinal data into information is two-fold: knowing what to extract and knowing how to display. Taking into account that customers not only value high performance, but also consistent, predictable services, the TRI*M-Six Sigma Plot combines the analysis of process performance with the variation in customer ratings. From this, not only areas of service and processes that do not meet customer needs can be identified; insight is also gained in how consistently the company is able to deliver products and services to its customers.

Displaying process performance versus consistency suggests where to start looking for improvement opportunities. Consistently low performance indicates a systematic problem: procedures and methods that, in general, are static may be a root cause. Any inconsistent (high variation) performance suggests that people, who are dynamic, are influencing the variation: training, leadership, working conditions, etc. might be areas to consider for improvement measures. With this, the TRI*M-Six Sigma Plot provides actionable insights and valuable information regarding where to look, what to fix, and what to exploit.

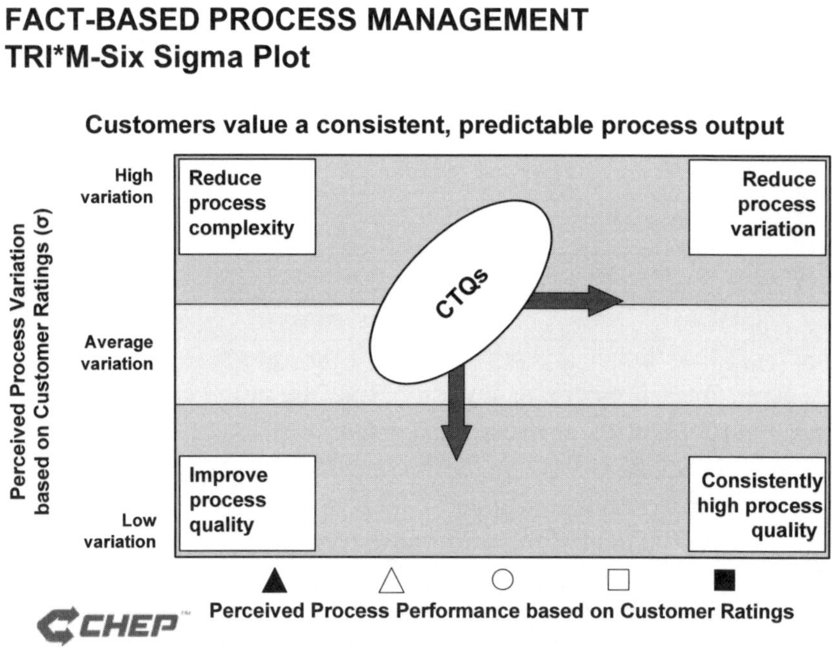

Fig. 7

The CHEP Canada 2003 analysis validates a strong correlation between the perceived process variation and process performance. Consistency at the customer touch-points leads to strong performance ratings and therefore drives overall customer retention. Customers expect high performance, and value reliability. However, they feel the variance in each transaction if a process does not meet their expectations.

Each dot on the chart represents a performance indicator of an individual process that is critical to customer retention.

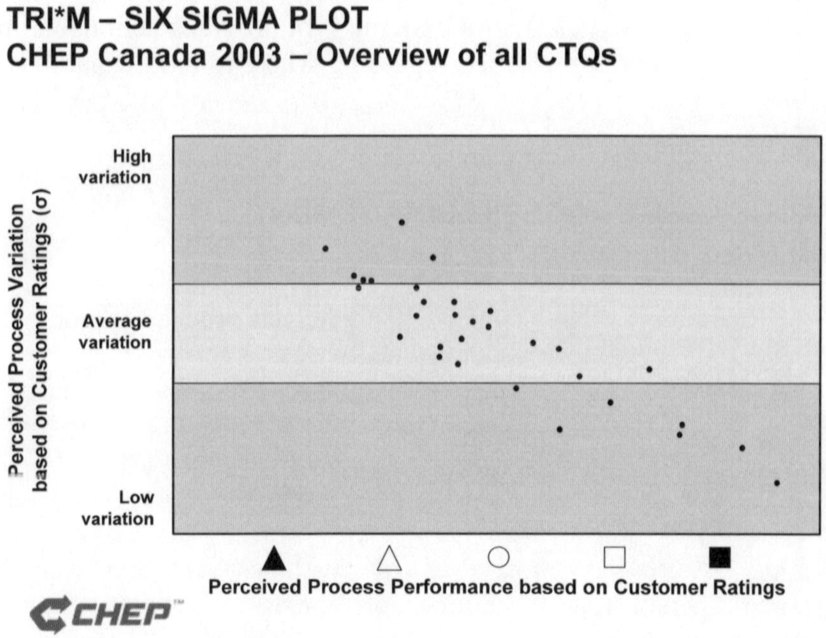

Fig. 8

Comparing the results of 2003 and 2004, a positive trend illustrates that overall perceived process variation decreased in 2004 where there were areas of Six Sigma focus. CHEP Canada's efforts to achieve stable operations and to drive continuous improvement ensures higher customer satisfaction on critical to quality attributes.

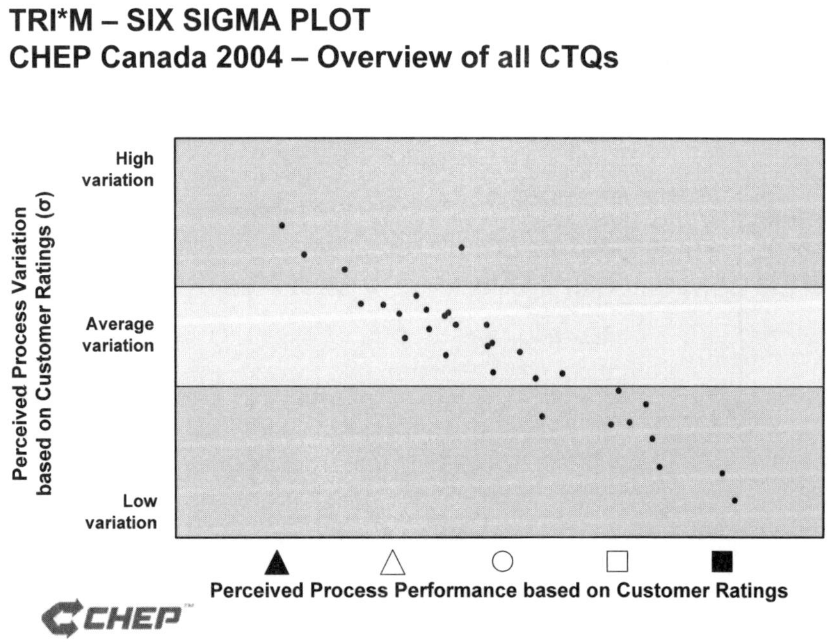

Fig. 9

Looking at the key motivators of customer retention from a customers' perspective, these processes operate on a weaker Sigma-level than all other customer processes. The analysis identifies for individual processes (i.e. D06) a strong need for process improvements. As described above, the TRI*M-Six Sigma Plot helps to review the processes and conduct root cause analysis, and thus supports the development of targeted improvement measures.

TRI*M – SIX SIGMA PLOT
CHEP Canada 2004 – Motivators only

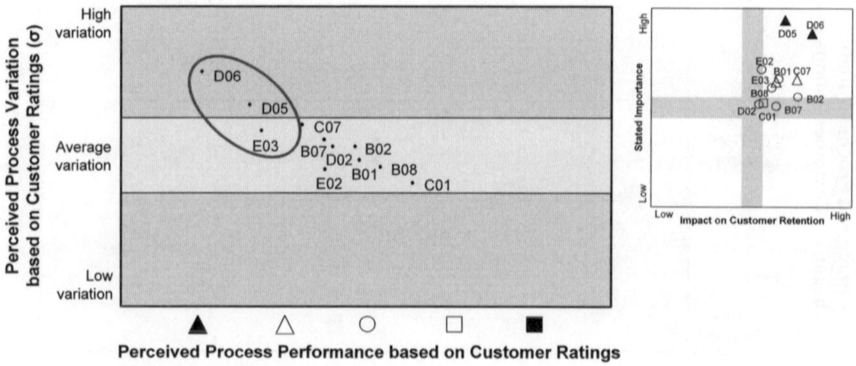

CHEP

Fig. 10

Conversely the charts can show the processes that have the lowest variation and operate on a well above average Sigma-level. As noted earlier, the TRI*M Index as a measure of the strength of customer retention has increased significantly in 2004. The TRI*M-Six Sigma analysis identifies issues Critical To Quality (CTQs), for which the process output is in line with customer expectations and needs. Therefore, CHEP Canada knows where to prioritize focus for further improvements and strengthen its market position.

TRI*M – SIX SIGMA PLOT
CHEP Canada 2004 – Processes with low variation

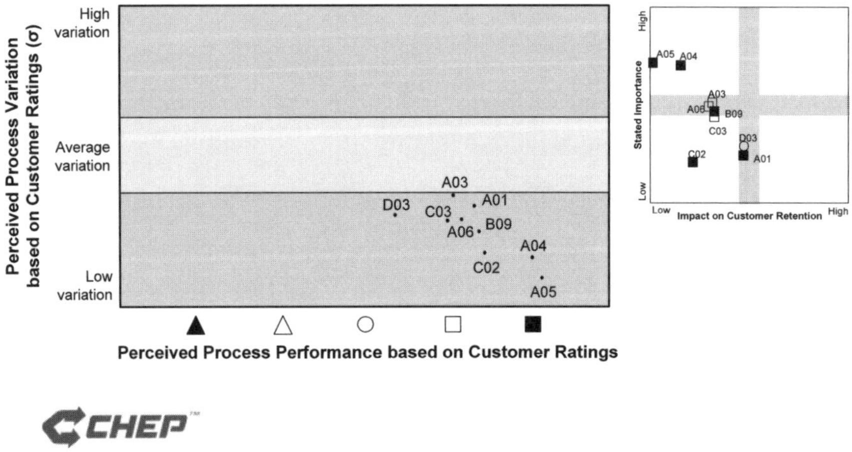

Fig. 11

Conclusion

Employing proven methodologies such as customer satisfaction and loyalty as measured by TRI*M with Six Sigma has the potential to provide focus on those attributes that are Critical to Quality. This will reduce variation, improve quality, improve customer satisfaction, increase customer retention, and provide the baseline for continuous improvement.

9 Focus on Loyalty

John Salusbury

Endress+Hauser is an international group of companies, offering process control devices and systems for all major parameters in industrial measurement and automation technologies. The Endress+Hauser Group maintains its own subsidiaries in all leading industrialised nations and has representatives in practically all other countries. Since the foundation in 1953, Endress+Hauser developed from being a specialist in level measurement, to a supplier of complete solutions for industrial measurement and automation. Proudly independent, the group is the largest privately owned process automation company in the world and is wholly owned by the Endress family.

Like many other companies, Endress+Hauser realised that only by consequent relationship development with its customers is it possible to have continued success on the long run. The challenges of today are many including: mature markets, rising competition, ambitious and price-conscious customers and products which are often viewed by the users as commodities. It's therefore important to focus on not just the product deliverables but also the relationship with the customers concentrating on the aspects of service which satisfy customers the most, to build trust and create loyalty. To achieve this long-lasting and profitable customer retention it was therefore recognised that Endress+Hauser had to regularly measure and analyse customer satisfaction.

Fig. 1

Not only is customer satisfaction stated as strategically important for the group it has been identified as one of the key and central objectives for company development. This is exemplified in the motto of the Endress+Hauser Group for 2003/ 2004 which was "Focus on Loyalty" and to quote the CEO Klaus Endress. "Loyalty is not about following someone blindly – but knowing that you can completely rely on your counterpart, that they are honest and trustworthy in their actions."[1]

[1] Citation of Klaus Endress, CEO of Endress+Hauser, 2004.

9.1 Loyalty Benefits Everyone – Loyalty Ensures Long-Term Success

A bridge made of nine multicoloured building blocks. One brick supports the other. Together they give each other support; collectively they form a strong bond – a long-lasting bond that is able to withstand a heavy burden. This simple analogy could not better illustrate the effect of loyal relations. This can be between companies on the one hand and customers, employees and shareholders on the other hand. (Reproduced from Changes 2004 the annual company report and magazine of the Endress+Hauser Group)

Fig. 2

It is not surprising to see in almost every corporate strategy the target to increase customer satisfaction which is influenced by their loyalty.

In 2000 one of the Product Centres (PC) of Endress+Hauser in Maulburg (Germany) decided to conduct a satisfaction survey to gain market feedback on one of their product groups. They selected TRI*M and the results gave insights on a number of aspects of the company's activities and in particular a view on customer satisfaction in relation to the products. This gave a focus on new developments ongoing at the time; the product was launched later in 2002 and has subsequently been proven a marketing success. Whilst the study pointed Endress+Hauser in the right direction it could also be noted that the products being produced at the time were voted as having very high quality, and viewed overall in a positive light.

In 2001 it was decided that not only did Endress+Hauser need to analyse their customers satisfaction with the products but they also needed to rate the satisfaction of customers in aspects of service beyond the product. Again Endress+Hauser decided to conduct the customer satisfaction survey with TNS Infratest using their TRI*M Methodology. The pilot project was carried out in the Sales Centre (SC) Switzerland. Whilst the survey by PC Maulburg focused on satisfaction in relation to the products, the second survey in SC Switzerland assessed customer satisfaction overall.

Endress+Hauser created in cooperation with TNS a master questionnaire adapted to the company structure. All Endress+Hauser companies have to use this master questionnaire to enable the group to benchmark the survey results afterwards. Of course, each country has the possibility to change items in the questionnaire, but generally this is less than 5 %. To change items it is necessary to observe the structure of the text in the master document. If an item is printed bold than it must not be changed. It has to be in the questionnaire like suggested. An italic printed item is recommended and should be included in the questionnaire if possible. A normal printed element is optional and can be changed or replaced by another item.

The following figure shows this in more detail:

How important are the following attributes in your opinion concerning „general company attributes“. **A General company attributes**	Extremely important =5	Very important =4	Fairly important =3	Not very important =2	Not at all important =1
A1 Market leader / Recognised brand	☐	☐	☐	☐	☐
A2 Worldwide presence	☐	☐	☐	☐	☐
A3 Provider of after sales service	☐	☐	☐	☐	☐
A4 Reliable partnership	☐	☐	☐	☐	☐
A5 Customer orientation	☐	☐	☐	☐	☐
A6 Innovative	☐	☐	☐	☐	☐
A7 Control system supplier	☐	☐	☐	☐	☐
A8 Technical and professional competence	☐	☐	☐	☐	☐

Fig. 3

Following another successful and informative telephone survey in the USA in 2003 Endress+Hauser decided to carry out further customer satisfaction surveys in 2004 in Austria, Germany and France. All three surveys were conducted at the same time. In 2005 the surveys where extended to include Canada, South Africa, United Kingdom, Denmark, Norway and Sweden. With the results out of the surveys in Europe, Africa and the USA it is again possible to benchmark different continents. With the results from Germany, Austria and France it is possible to verify if there are any regional coherencies or not.

With this special master questionnaire it is possible to benchmark results of Endress+Hauser companies from all over the world against each other but also more importantly by using the historical data of TNS to benchmark Endress+Hauser against similar organisations operating in the same regions. Next steps will to conduct further surveys in Europe but in 2006 extend the approach to Japan and South East Asia.

9.2 Customer Satisfaction Survey in Europe

Endress+Hauser Germany, Austria and France decided to again take advantage of telephone surveys. Despite the increased costs of this method the companies could see a great advantage in getting feedback directly from the nominated target person or target group in a very short period of time. Both would be more difficult to control and guaranteed using the mail survey. To get representative results it is important to select the right customers. Of course, this requires a complete, maintained and accurate customer database.

Within the scope of the survey Endress+Hauser defined the focus groups on which they required feedback. Germany preferred on the one hand to ask mainly A and B Customers. These customers are equally listed with commercial and technical contact persons to enable a more detailed differentiation. On the other hand they focused obtaining information across customers of different branches to obtain a more detailed view on their customer retention in main focal industries. (A and B category customers tend to be the bigger users of Endress+Hauser products and offer the potential for continued business development).

Endress+Hauser Austria had a preference to view their results from a regional perspective. As one sales person is responsible for one region and additionally each of them is accountable for about one to two key customers, the feeling was that the survey could help each sales person to develop and improve his area based on the strengths and weaknesses perceived by the customers. Endress+Hauser Austria also received the anonymous but separate results of each key customer.

The customer selection by Endress+Hauser France was similar to Austria. Additional to the A-B &C-customers of each region they wanted to have the results more divided in application areas and different branches of their customers. This was achieved in an excellent way and despite the short Fieldwork of only 3 weeks it was possible to fulfil all five criteria France requested. This on the one side showed that the customer database was in a very good condition and the on the other that customers are willing to participate to the survey.

For future surveys Endress+Hauser will continue to use such Methodology to look at their business from different aspects that are aligned to their strategic targets. The following figure highlights this approach in more detail. By identifying the focal business area on the customer database that is submitted to TNS prior to the survey it is possible to guide the interviewers to get completed questionnaires within the business group required.

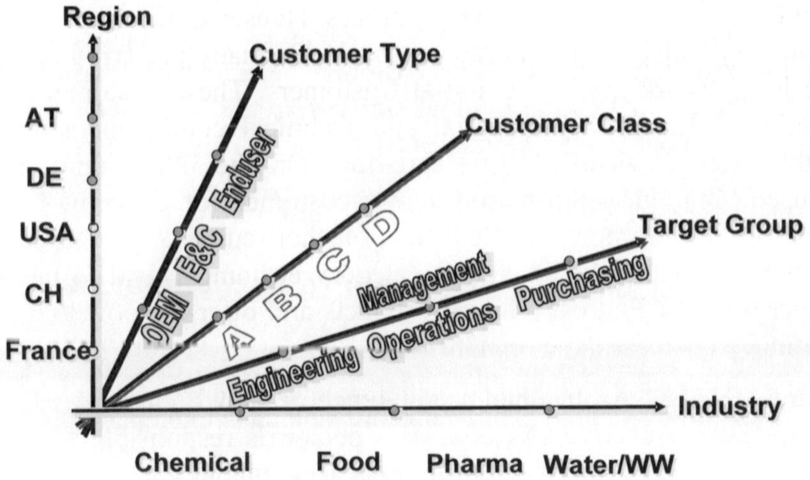

Fig. 4

After each survey or group of surveys a workshop was conducted with TNS with an analysis of the results and a specific focus into the strength and weaknesses as reported by customers. These workshops allowed Endress+Hauser to analyse on the one hand each country's activities where they have to focus on to improve in their region. On the other hand with the combined benchmarked results of all surveys Endress+Hauser were able to isolate the customer perceived strengths and weaknesses which are in relation to the group of companies. This has resulted in several group projects aimed at improving communication to users of strengths and also two projects to tackle two areas where improvement of company performance will enhance satisfaction and gain a competitive advantage in comparison to other suppliers of automation products.

With the accomplishment of satisfaction surveys with TNS Infratest to date and on the strength of the information delivered, the acceptance of the TRI*M Methodology is high within the Endress+ Hauser group companies. TRI*M Methodology along with TNS will be employed further on by Endress+Hauser for future external studies. The nature of the questioning techniques will be developed and in 2006 it is envisaged that a number of hybrid surveys can be carried out combining on line questionnaires with focussed telephone surveys towards the key customer personnel. The aim is to reduce the cost of the individual surveys so that the Methodology can be rolled out to all major sales centres of Endress+Hauser.

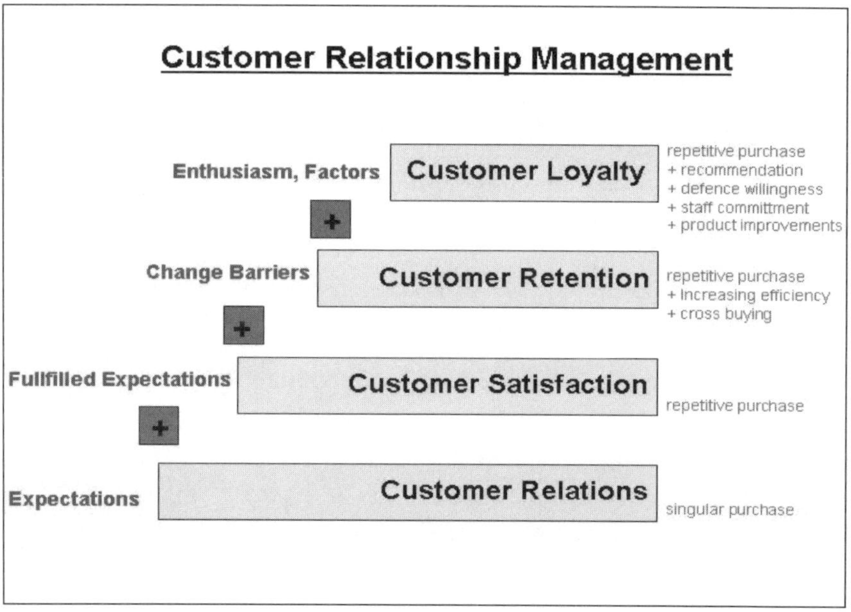

Fig. 5

10 The Customer as Process Manager: Utilization of the TRI*M Methodology to Continually Increase Customer Satisfaction

Anja Regnat, Fabian Schwarz

10.1 PAYBACK – Germany's Largest Customer Retention Programme

Collecting bonus points when making a purchase has become almost a habit for the consumers in Germany. With over 28 million cards currently deployed, PAYBACK - Germany's leading bonus programme - has greatly contributed towards this trend; and done so within a very short period of time. The PAYBACK-brand was launched as the first ever multi-partner-bonus programme by Loyalty Partner GmbH in March 2000. Ever since this point in time, PAYBACK-members are able to collect bonus points from a multitude of sales and service companies.

Through PAYBACK, Loyalty Partner have established themselves to be the most successful providers of bonus programmes. The "success formula" is simple and complex at the same time: All processes should be customer-oriented. All programme-relevant areas such as "registration", "collection" and "redemption", as well as the service beyond these processes, should be included in this task.

The complexity lies in the multitude of existing part-processes inherent for the running of the individual programme areas. The process of collecting, for example, contains over 64 sub-processes computing up to 4 million transactions a day and managing all accounts via a complex account-management-system. These highly automated sub-processes run million-fold and are controlled by high-performance monitoring tools.

Despite the process-complexity, PAYBACK remains a programme that is easily manageable for the customer and responds analogous to its core idea: "To collect points from all partners with just one card". The ease of use is an essential prerequisite for the acceptance and usage of the PAYBACK-programme - just as a perfect service can only generate complete customer satisfaction if its approach remains straightforward.

A closer look at customer satisfaction can indicate insufficiencies in the alignment of company-related processes with the customer and is therefore an immediate indicator for customer retention. Given this criteria, it is not surprising that customer satisfaction is the central entrepreneurial goal of Loyalty Partner. The overall success of the PAYBACK-programme depends to a great deal on it.

10.2 The Core Indicator for Customer Retention: The Measurement of the Customer Satisfaction in the Customer Service Centre

In order to safeguard and to continually increase customer retention, in 2003 Loyalty Partner conducted the measurement of customer satisfaction with the Customer Service Centre for the first time. The aim of the initial measurement was the assessment of all individual customer-related processes of the PAYBACK-programme through the measurement of the overall service processes. The attainment of the customer's viewpoint should enable the alignment and the improvement of the programme with the requirements of the customer.

10.2.1 Selection of the TRI*M Methodology and the Suitable Research Design

For the selection of an appropriate measurement tool, the requirements were clearly defined before conducting the initial measurement. Customer satisfaction should be measured in such a way that it is:

- valid und reliable
- comparable (benchmarking)

- including individual relevance of different target groups
- containing all contact channels (call, letter, email)

Additionally, the tool had to be accepted by all stakeholders and integrable into the Balanced Scorecard of the company.

In order to meet the aforementioned requirements for the measurement tool, Loyalty Partner chose the TRI*M methodology from TNS Infratest. The decision for this methodology was easy: Even before commencing with the regular measurement of customer satisfaction, this methodology proved successful in the context of other company-wide studies.

The structuring of an adequate research design for selecting a suitable sample proved to be more of an effort. Existing statistics of the PAYBACK Service Centre were analysed according to volume, frequency and contact channels. A sample, representing the following areas, had to be generated:

- Organisational structure of the Service Centre regarding share of workload (front office, back office)
- Different contact channels (call, letter, email) as well as their significance regarding volume
- Handling of queries and complaints and their respective significance for the overall customer satisfaction
- Different levels of complaint handling (initial complaint / repeat complaint / complaint escalation)

The intended sample, therefore, represented three levels of complaint handling, encompassing three target groups in accordance to contact channels. The handling of queries and complaints could be analysed separately. Through weighing according to the proportion of queries and complaints, an overall value for customer satisfaction could be identified. The performance for all target groups was established through the TRI*M Index and was therefore easily comparable.

As the customer is being asked to remember a certain point in time in the past regarding an incident or service, it is essential that only those are selected whose contact with the Customer Service Centre has been just a few days or weeks ago.

10.2.2 Results of the Initial Measurement 2003

The results of the initial measurement in 2003 were of a mixed nature: The customer satisfaction for the whole Customer Service Centre was near the benchmark set by TNS Infratest and thus assessed as 'competitive with potential for improvement'. With regards to the contact channels, the TRI*M Index for the handling of telephone queries was very positive; the handling of written queries (letter or email), however, was below average. The overall handling of queries was dealt with to the satisfaction of the customers for the most part. The handling of complaints, however, indicated a lot of room for improvement: All three satisfaction levels were of a low standard; in one case the TRI*M Index was below zero (see illustration: Extracts of index values).

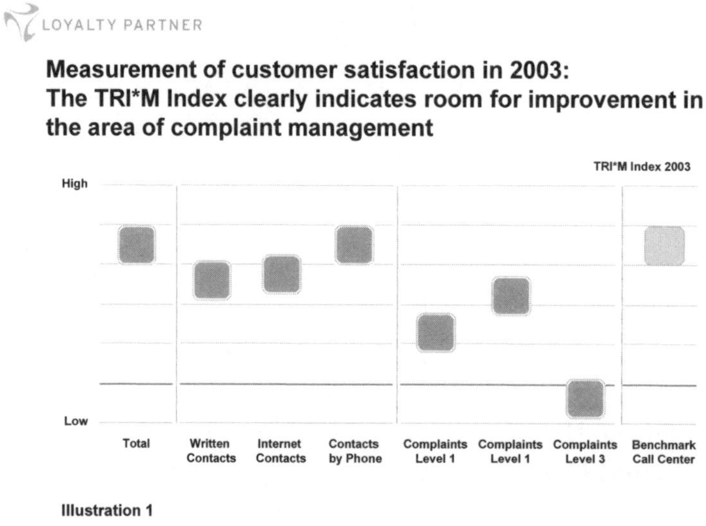

Fig. 1

The Strengths-Weaknesses analysis through the TRI*M Grid indicates clear starting points for the improvement of complaint handling - particularly in the field of Motivators (see illustration).

From a customer's viewpoint, the following aspects show up in particular: "Response addresses the issue in question", "Reliable information", "Competent response", "Reliable Statements" and "Promises are kept".

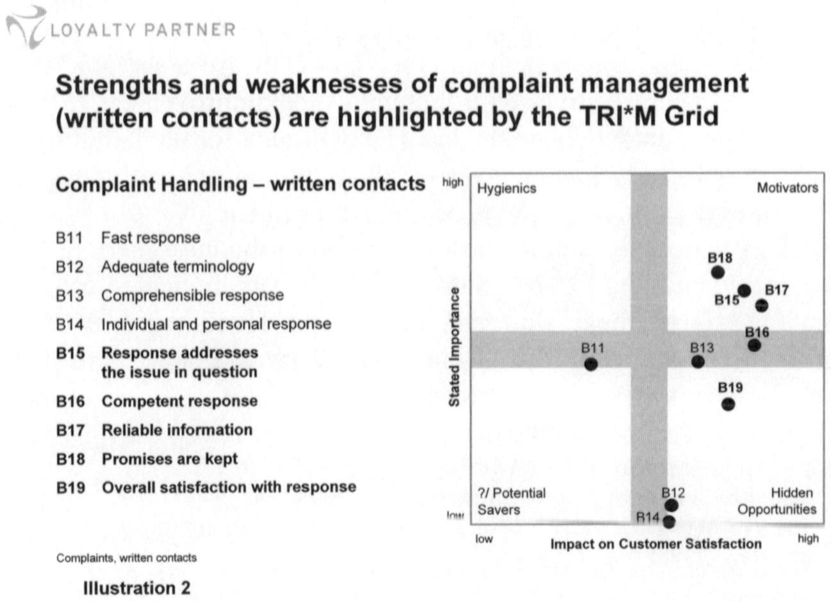

Fig. 2

Aspects relating to the performance of the agents in the Service Centre ("courtesy", "friendliness" and "comprehensibility of the agent"), were evaluated by the customer as far above average.

10.2.3 Analysis and Optimization of the Before Mentioned Processes

The results indicated that during the process of definition and implementation of improvement measures, special attention should be given to the area of complaint management. First recommendations by TNS Infratest instigated an extensive process analysis by Loyalty Partner.

In the context of the analysis, it became apparent that the actual core problem was not the serviceability of the Customer Service Centre, but its integration into the overall programme. In many respects, the agents could not supply satisfactory solutions to the customers because:

- There were no encompassing organizational structures for controlling the Service Centre in place
- There was not enough information / knowledge management put into practice
- There was a lack of process know-how or a lack of insight into the processes by the Service Centre
- There was no adequate system support

On the basis of these findings, the company-wide project, "The customer as focal point" was launched. With this project, a clear shift in perspective took place, namely from the operational viewpoint to the perspective of the customer. Improvement measures were initiated in the following four areas:

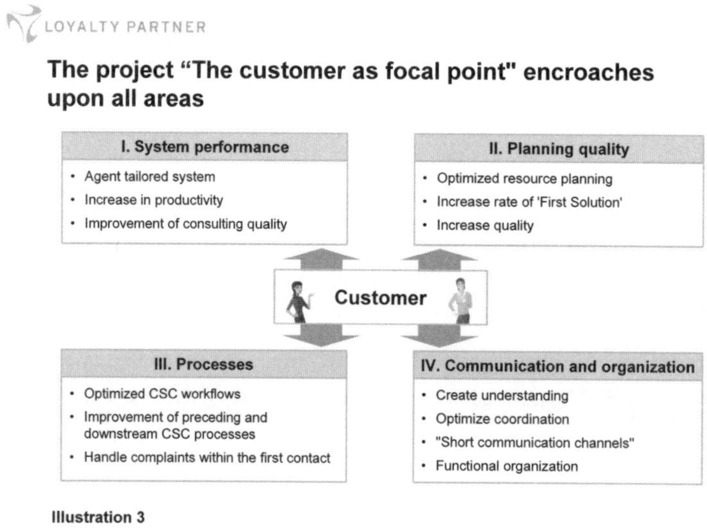

Fig. 3

The project could only be made a success because of the strong commitment of the management. Furthermore, it was necessary to realize that the close-knit link between the service and the operational side of the programme provides the prerequisite for satisfied customers. Because, only if the agent of the PAYBACK Service Centre feels as a part of the overall programme and shows his/her satisfaction, he/she will be able to affect the customer in the same fashion.

10.2.4 Measurement of Customer Satisfaction 2004

The results of the customer satisfaction survey 2004 confirmed the chosen path:

For each target group examined, improvements could be registered by means of higher index values. The overall TRI*M Index was increased by 6 index points, the performance by different contact channels by 5 to 11 index points.

A tremendous success was achieved with regards to handling complaints:

Customer satisfaction for the first complaint level was improved by 24 index points in 2004. For repeat complaints, it was improved by 18 index points.

Complaint escalations occurred less in 2004 than in the previous year and only few customers could be interviewed. However, these customers were clearly more satisfied with the handling of their complaint (Improvement by 49 index points).

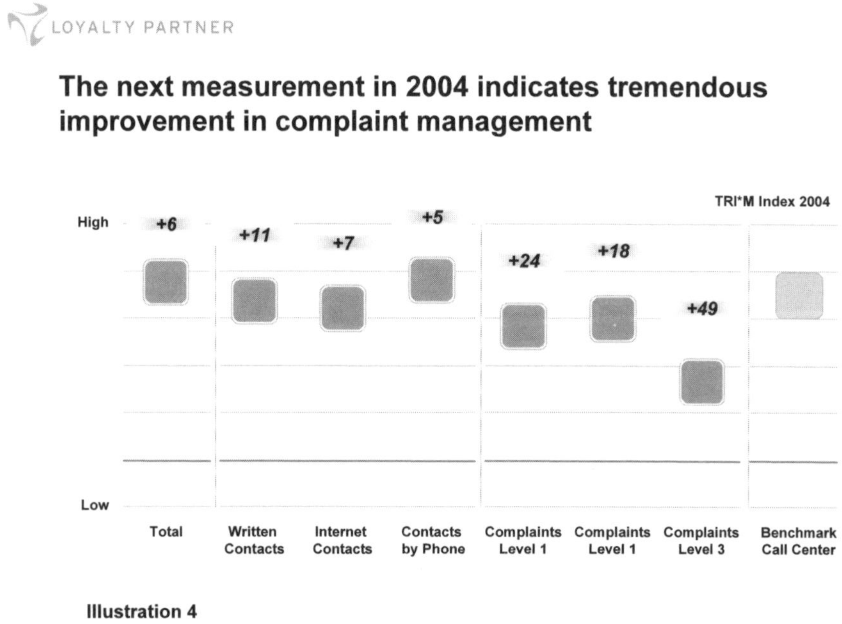

Fig. 4

10.3 Regular Utilization of the TRI*M Results in Order to Derive Measures to Increase Customer Satisfaction

The success, which has been achieved through the measurement of the customer satisfaction in the Customer Service Centre within one year, has prompted the company to measure on an annual basis. This means that every year, the customer of the PAYBACK Service Centre is given indirectly the role of a process manager, who contributes to the continual improvement in customer satisfaction.

LOYALTY PARTNER

The processes to increase customer satisfaction need to be continually driven:

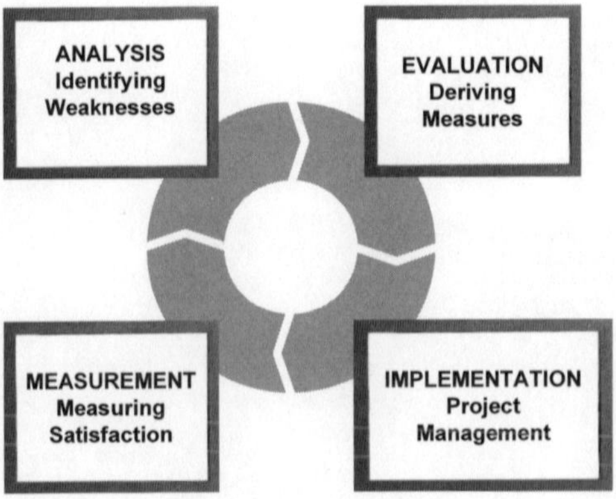

Illustration 5

Fig. 5

The TRI*M methodology has proved itself when it comes to measurement, management and further development of customer satisfaction. And as such, supports Loyalty Partner's 'success formula', to offer through PAYBACK a product that has all its processes aligned with the customer.

Authors

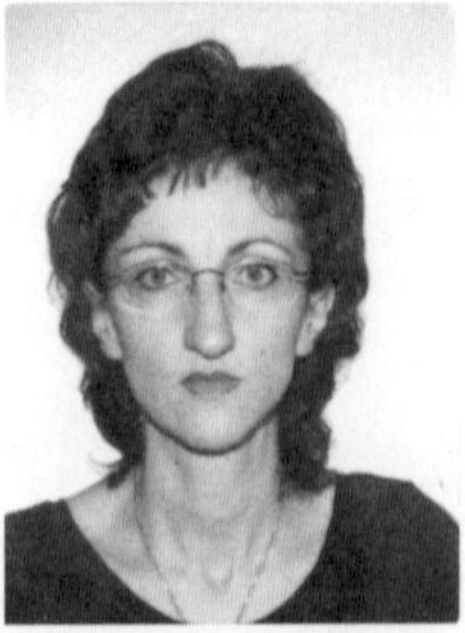

Zuzana Heleyová is Information Group Manager of Plzensky Prazdroj, a.s. (SAB Miller) - with responsibility of Czech and Slovak Republics. She is in charge for the applied knowledge management in both markets, leading the research and analysts team.

Chapter 6

Dr. Margit Huber, Business Area Manager at TNS Infratest is responsible for international market research surveys, especially in the area of Customer Satisfaction in the B2B Industry and Employee Commitment. In addition, she is in charge of the group's network of more than 250 consultants working in the area of Stakeholder Management.

Chapter 2

Lynnette Leathers has worked for notable multinational corporations like Kellogg's, British American Tobacco as well as CHEP, her current employer. She manages global marketing and customer satisfaction research for the company's 300,000 pallet and container management customers in 42 countries. Leathers is Vice President of Marketing for the Central Florida Chapter of the American Marketing Association (AMA) and holds a BSBA from Montana State University and an MBA from the University of Montana.

Chapter 8

Oliver Lucas is a consultant at TNS. Since 2002 he has been consulting with retail clients to help them optimise their in-store experience and marketing communications. The use of TRI*M has formed a critical part of CRM programme implementation.

Chapter 1

Dr. Susanne O'Gorman is Key Account Manager for Loyalty Partner and responsible for Hotline Consultancy at the Global TRI*M Centre. Currently she mainly focuses on Customer Retention and the development of ISQ and Process Analysis. Before that she worked for over six year at TNS Infratest InCom as a director in the Telecommunications Market. Susanne did a degree in Sociology at the University of Regensburg. After a stay at the London School of Economics she finalised her PhD at the University of Regensburg.

Chapter 7

Dr. Peter Pirner is responsible for the business area commercial vehicles and works as sector champion for Stakeholder Management at TNS Infratest Automotive. Before that he worked as international consulting executive for Stakeholder Management at the Global TRI*M Centre. Peter focused strongly on the development and marketing of the TRI*M business solution "Corporate Reputation Manager". Peter earned a PhD in Economics and a master in Business Administration from Munich University.

Chapter 7

Anja Regnat is head of market research of Loyalty Partner, expert in field of customer management, in Munich. She is responsible for all market research surveys, the main focus being customer retention and employee satisfaction studies. Before that she worked for 5 years as project manager in market research institutes.

Chapter 10

John Salusbury's present position is Director Asset Management Solutions within corporate management of Endress+Hauser, based in Switzerland. He started his career in the UK with British Steel serving a four year apprenticeship in Instrumentation combined with studies at the North Wales Institute resulting in a diploma in Industrial Measurement and Control. As an Instrument Engineer he has worked for various companies including ICI, Sasol, Shell and Kraft foods.

Chapter 9

Dr. Joachim Scharioth is Managing Director of TNS Infratest, a subsidiary of TNS. He is responsible for the Group's offering in the Stakeholder Management area worldwide.

He has published an array of research articles and papers in the Stakeholder Management area over the last 15 years.

Chapter 2

Michael Schroth has studied Business Administration at the TH-Darmstadt as well as the J.-W.-Goethe-University in Frankfurt. He has worked for 4 years in the marketing department at Bausparkasse Schwäbisch Hall, for 2 years as head of the market research department at Telenorma (TN) and for 2 years as a department head for Marplan Forschungsgesellschaft. He has worked as the head of the market research department at Commerzbank since 1984.

Chapter 5

Fabian Schwarz is Customer Service Manager at PAYBACK, Germany's largest and most successful loyalty programme. He is responsible for the entire service side of the business, the creation of customer friendly processes and the integration of customer trends into the business. Beforehand he worked as a process manager in the tourism and airline industry.

Chapter 10

Christine Theodorovics has been the head of Quality Mangement at Swiss Life since 2004. She is responsible for improving the internal and external service quality and designing customer-oriented processes with the aid of Six Sigma. Holding degrees from the Wirtschaftsuniversität in Vienna as well as from the European College in Brussels, she is also an alumnus of the Executive Programs of the Swiss Banking School.

Chapter 3

Phil Tysoe, General Manager Commercial Information, is responsible for all customer insight and market research at Comet Group Plc, part of the pan-European electricals group, KESA. Beginning his career at Boots The Chemists he has held a variety of Marketing roles before taking on his current position in 2001. Following the successful introduction of TRI*M and Stakeholder Management principles to the business, he is now working on driving operational change through ongoing customer measurement.

Chapter 1

Mandy Littlewood is a Managing Consultant based in Edinburgh. She joined TNS in May 1998 from the Centre for Housing Research and Urban Studies at Glasgow University, where she was a Research Fellow. Mandy has a first class honours degree in Sociology. She has directed a wide range of housing research projects. Mandy has designed and managed a number of tenants and residents surveys incorporating TRI*M to identify residents' service priorities.

Chapter 4

Anna Dudleston (Managing Consultant) joined TNS in 1999 from Nottingham Trent University where she was studying for a PhD examining the inter-relationships between the housing and labour markets. She has a degree in Social Policy and Administration from the University of Nottingham. Anna has recently managed studies on homelessness strategy and housing affordability as well as the TRI*M residents survey on which this paper is based.

Chapter 4

Printing: Krips bv, Meppel, The Netherlands
Binding: Stürtz, Würzburg, Germany